Best Hikes Colorado's Front Range

HELP US KEEP THIS GUIDE UP TO DATE

Every effort has been made by the author and editors to make this guide as accurate and useful as possible. However, many things can change after a guide is published—regulations change, facilities come under new management, and so forth.

We would love to hear from you concerning your experiences with this guide and how you feel it could be improved and kept up to date. While we may not be able to respond to all comments and suggestions, we'll take them to heart, and we'll also make certain to share them with the author. Please send your comments and suggestions to falconeditorial@rowman.com.

Thanks for your input!

Best Hikes Colorado's Front Range

Simple Strolls, Day Hikes, and Longer Adventures

Abbie Mood

FALCONGUIDES

ESSEX, CONNECTICUT

FALCONGUIDES®

An imprint of Globe Pequot, the trade division of The Rowman & Littlefield Publishing Group, Inc.
4501 Forbes Blvd., Ste. 200
Lanham, MD 20706
www.rowman.com
Falcon and FalconGuides are registered trademarks and Make Adventure Your Story is a trademark
of The Rowman & Littlefield Publishing Group, Inc.

Distributed by NATIONAL BOOK NETWORK

Copyright © 2024 The Rowman & Littlefield Publishing Group, Inc.

All photos by Abbie Mood unless noted otherwise
Maps by The Rowman & Littlefield Publishing Group, Inc.

British Library Cataloguing in Publication Information available

Library of Congress Cataloging-in-Publication Data available
Names: Mood, Abbie, author.
Title: Best hikes Colorado's Front Range : simple strolls, day hikes, and
    longer adventures / Abbie Mood.
Description: Essex, Connecticut : Falcon Guides, [2024] | Includes index.
Identifiers: LCCN 2023050734 (print) | LCCN 2023050735 (ebook) | ISBN
    9781493066889 (trade paperback) | ISBN 9781493066896 (epub)
Subjects: LCSH: Hiking–Colorado–Guidebooks. |
    Trails–Colorado–Guidebooks. | Front Range (Colo. and
    Wyo.)–Guidebooks. | BISAC: SPORTS & RECREATION / Hiking | LCGFT:
    Guidebooks.
Classification: LCC GV199.42.C62 F676 2024 (print) | LCC GV199.42.C62
    (ebook) | DDC 796.5109788/6–dc23/eng/20231115
LC record available at https://lccn.loc.gov/2023050734
LC ebook record available at https://lccn.loc.gov/2023050735

∞™ The paper used in this publication meets the minimum requirements of American National
Standard for Information Sciences—Permanence of Paper for Printed Library Materials, ANSI/NISO
Z39.48-1992.

Contents

Acknowledgments viii

Meet Your Guide ix

Introduction xi

    Geologic History xiii

    Flora and Fauna xiv

    Weather xviii

    Summer Storms xix

    Altitude Sickness xix

    Hiking with Dogs xx

    Trail Etiquette xxi

How to Use This Guide xxiii

How to Use the Maps xxv

Trail Finder xxvi

Map Legend xxviii

Fort Collins Area 1

  1 Horsetooth Falls Loop 3

  2 Devil's Backbone Loop 9

  A Lory State Park 14

  B Poudre River Trail 15

Rocky Mountain National Park **16**

  3 Dream and Emerald Lakes Trail 18

  4 Lake Haiyaha Loop 22

  5 Ouzel Falls via Wild Basin Trail 27

  6 Finch Lake via Allenspark Trail 31

Boulder Area **35**

  7 Davidson Mesa Open Space 37

  8 Walker Ranch Loop 41

  9 Royal Arch Trail 46

 10 Sugarloaf Mountain 52

 11 Wapiti and Ponderosa Loop Trails 55

 12 Caribou Ranch Loop 60

 13 Lake Isabelle via Pawnee Pass Trail 65

 14 Ceran St. Vrain Trail to Miller Rock 71

 15 Crater Lakes via South Boulder Creek Trail 76

 16 Rattlesnake Gulch Trail—Eldorado Canyon State Park 81

 17 Flatirons Vista Trail 85

  C Green Mountain via Gregory Canyon and Ranger Trails 89

  D Lost Lake via Hessie Trail 90

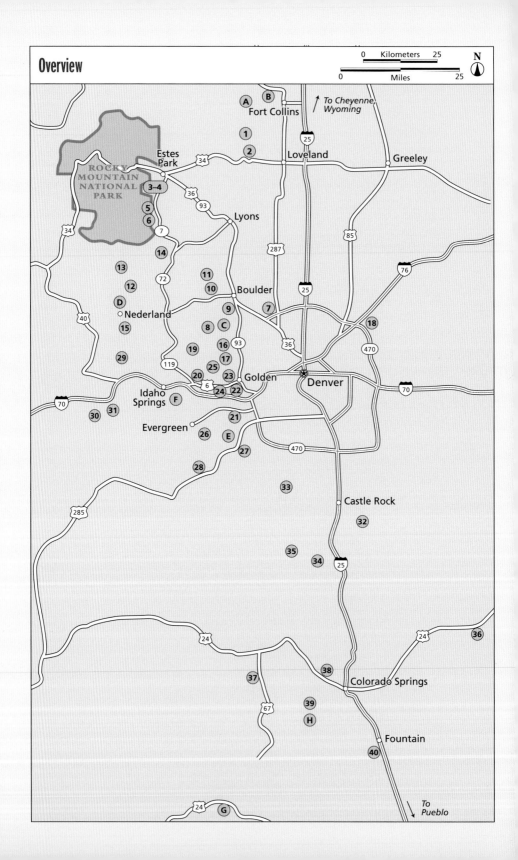

Overview

0 Kilometers 25

0 Miles 25

N

A B
Fort Collins

→ To Cheyenne, Wyoming

1

2 Loveland

Greeley

34

36

93

Lyons

287

ROCKY MOUNTAIN NATIONAL PARK

Estes Park

3–4

5

6

7

34

25

85

14

13

72

11

10 Boulder

76

12

D Nederland

9 7

8 C

18

40

15

93

36

470

19 16

17

29

119 25

20 23 Golden

6 24 22

Denver

70

Idaho Springs F

30 31

21

Evergreen

26 E

27

28

470

33

285

Castle Rock

32

35

34 25

24

36

24

37

38 Colorado Springs

67

39

H

Fountain

40

24 G

→ To Pueblo

Denver Area **91**

18 Barr Lake Loop—Barr Lake State Park 93
19 Raccoon Trail—Golden Gate Canyon State Park 97
20 Beaver Brook and Chavez Trail Loop 102
21 Mount Falcon Park Upper Loop 107
22 Dakota Ridge Trail 113
23 Mount Galbraith Loop via Cedar Gulch Trail 117
24 Peaks to Plains Trail—Gateway Trailhead 122
25 Belcher Hill and Mustang Trails 126
26 Evergreen Mountain Trail 131
27 Sunny Aspen Trail and Lodge Pole Loop 135
28 Staunton Ranch, Old Mill, and Border Line Trails—Staunton
    State Park 138
29 St. Mary's Glacier and James Peak 144
30 Grays and Torreys Peaks 148
31 South Park 600 Trail to Square Top Lakes 154
32 Castlewood Canyon State Park Loops 158
33 South Rim and Willow Creek Trails—Roxborough State Park ... 163
34 Sandstone Meadow Loop 168
35 Devil's Head Lookout Trail 172
 E O'Fallon Park Loop 178
 F Bergen Peak 179

Colorado Springs Area **180**

36 Paint Mines Interpretive Park 182
37 Lost Pond Loop—Mueller State Park 186
38 Susan G. Bretag and Palmer Loop 191
39 Palmer Trail (Section 16) 196
40 Fountain Creek Nature Trail 202
 G Royal Gorge Canyon Rim 205
 H Mount Muscoco Trail 205

Local Resources and Groups 206
Hike Index 208

Acknowledgments

This guidebook wouldn't have been possible without more than a few people. First, my partner Jacob, who was by my side every step of the way—literally and figuratively. Thank you for your endless support, motivation, and love. And thank you to Martha Goodrich for your words of encouragement and understanding while I was finishing up this guide.

A huge thanks to Dr. James Genuario, Jeremy Smith, Ali (Laura) Nabers, and the rest of the fantastic team at the UCHealth Steadman Hawkins Clinic Denver. You all got my hip back in tip-top shape so that I could not only enjoy life, but enjoy hiking again.

I'm thankful for some great friends who lent words of encouragement throughout this entire process: James Dziezynski and Emma Walker for your guidebook mentorship, Emily Gibson for your constant encouragement, Shannon Connor for your support, and Connor Cape for reminding me that it's okay to slow down and enjoy the hike instead of rushing to get to the destination.

A note of gratitude to my parents, who encouraged me and my brother to play outside, get in the dirt, and appreciate activities that allowed us to experience nature. I don't know if I would've been inspired to see what else was out there otherwise.

Thank you to the entire team at the Rowman & Littlefield Publishing Group. So many people were involved in making this guidebook happen, and I'm grateful for all of your expertise and contributions.

And, of course, thank you to all of the volunteers and organizations who help make these trails accessible for us to enjoy.

Meet Your Guide

Abbie has always been an explorer at heart—whether it was playing in the woods or looking for tadpoles in creeks near her grandparents' house—so it was only natural that she look for a bigger playground after graduating from college in her home state of Delaware. And so, Abbie picked up and moved across the country to California, where she found a love for hiking, climbing, and camping. In search of even more outdoor adventure, she moved to Colorado in 2011. Now Abbie lives for long summer days of hiking in the Front Range with her partner and their dogs. She enjoys both easy walks and more challenging trails and has summited a handful of 14ers over the years.

Abbie is a freelance writer and content marketing expert who has written for *Backpacker, Sierra, Yoga Journal,* and other publications. She loves sharing people's stories and shedding light on organizations that are making a difference. Learn more about Abbie on her website at abbiemood.com and follow along with her hiking adventures on Instagram @frontrangehikes.

JACOB PREBLE

During the heat of the summer, just before sunset is a perfect time to hit many of the Front Range trails.

Introduction

Colorado is a haven for people who love the outdoors. From rugged mountains and wildflower-filled meadows to alpine lakes and raging rivers, there is no shortage of places worth exploring. Heck, plenty of people here love to simply enjoy our 300-plus days of sunshine on a rooftop patio, taking in views of the Rockies in the distance.

Whether you're a paddler, climber, mountain biker, hiker, or anything in between, there is something for you in the Centennial State. When it comes to hiking, in particular, there are seemingly endless options, and the Front Range is one of the best places to start.

Geographically speaking, Colorado's Front Range is essentially the "Front" of the Rocky Mountains, running from the state's border with Wyoming in the north down to the town of Pueblo in the south, sitting west of the major cities of Fort Collins, Boulder, Denver, and Colorado Springs. From there, many locals will say the Front Range is essentially the foothills of the Rockies that are easily accessible from town, especially Denver; however, the region technically goes west until the Continental Divide. The Continental Divide splits the state in two from north to south, with water west of the divide running to the Pacific Ocean and water east of the divide running to the Gulf of Mexico and Atlantic Ocean. With the exception of Rabbit Ears Pass en route to Steamboat Springs, the Continental Divide sits above 10,000 feet in elevation.

Most of the hikes in this book fall into the foothills category that locals would be most familiar with, but no "best hikes" book that covers the Front Range would be complete without including a few that push to the outer reaches of the Continental Divide, offering incredible mountain views, unbelievably blue alpine lakes, and interesting abandoned mining sites. Conversely, there are also a couple options that sit a little farther east than I-25 (the unofficial eastern boundary of the Front Range) but are worth seeing if you're in or near the area.

Hike starting points range from just over 5,000 feet in elevation all the way up to 14,270 feet, though most fall within the 6,000- to 8,000-foot range. You'll have the opportunity to experience a variety of flora and fauna, including aspens, Douglas firs, spruce, cottonwoods, ponderosa and lodgepole pines, and more. Bright bursts of wildflowers contrast low-lying shrubs, cacti, and yuccas. A wide range of wildlife makes their home on these lands, including mountain lions, coyotes, bighorn sheep, moose, deer, elk, bald and golden eagles, yellow-bellied marmots, American pikas, squirrels, chipmunks, and many, many more.

It is a daunting task to narrow down hundreds of options to the best, and I fully acknowledge that this list is mostly subjective. I've included a handful of hikes that you simply must add to a roundup like this, but the reality is that many of these trails already have high foot traffic that limits access. In an effort to introduce some similarly

Some trails cross over grazing lands, so give cows the same respect and space that you'd give wildlife.

fantastic hikes, many others were chosen because they have something unique to offer, like dinosaur tracks, access to the only full-time fire lookout left in the state, or an unusual rock formation. Each hike in this book is within about an hour's drive (often less) from the closest major city.

I hope you use this book as a guide to places where you can calm your mind, breathe the fresh air, and maybe even see some wildlife along the way. There may be moments where your lungs and legs will burn, but I promise it will be worth it. You'll come away with a deeper knowledge of the area, and the opportunity to connect more closely and experience more fully the wonders these lands offer. I also want to respectfully acknowledge that this book covers the traditional land of Indigenous peoples, including the Arapaho, Southern Ute and Ute Mountain, Cheyenne, Lakota, Apache, Kiowa, and Comanche. Those of us who spend hours upon hours enjoying these trails have a responsibility to honor those who once lived here, respect the land and its current inhabitants, and do our best to follow the "Leave No Trace" principles so that future generations can experience the same beauty that you see before you today.

Enjoy every moment out there!

The view of Red Rocks Park from atop Dakota Ridge.

Geologic History

Even before the Rocky Mountains as we know them today were formed, the Ancestral Rocky Mountains existed. They consisted of two mountain ranges: the Uncompahgria and the Frontrangia. The former is around where the Uncompahgre Plateau sits in western Colorado, and the latter is—you guessed it—where the Front Range sits today. But the landscape looked a little different 300-plus million years ago: Colorado was near the equator as part of the Pangea supercontinent, and Uncompahgria and Frontrangia were mountainous islands, rising out of the shallow Western Interior Seaway. Over time, the rocks eroded and were deposited throughout the state to form some of our iconic landmarks: the Flatirons in Boulder, Red Rocks Park and Roxborough State Park in Denver, and Garden of the Gods in Colorado Springs.

Over time, the Ancestral Rocky Mountains eroded to sea level, and by 150 million years ago, the state looked more like Louisiana or Mississippi. During the Cretaceous period, dinosaurs thrived, including the state dinosaur, the stegosaurus. The rivers that crisscrossed Colorado deposited shale and sandstone that make up the Morrison Formation, just west of Denver and famous for its fossil deposits. Many

> The hogback formations in the Front Range are easy to spot: they are long, narrow, bumpy ridges with one steep side and one sloping side. (They kind of look like the back of the state dinosaur, the stegosaurus!) Hogbacks are formed when a sedimentary formation lifts and tilts the layers; then, the softer layers are eroded more quickly than the harder layers, which is what causes the two different sides. Over time, the characteristics become more pronounced, especially the steep, jagged side.

well-known dinosaur species, including the stegosaurus and apatosaurus, were first discovered in the Morrison Formation. Eventually, the sea began flooding the state and the Front Range became the eastern shoreline, resulting in the Dakota Hogback Formation west of Denver.

The continent continued to shift north until 75 million years ago, when it reached its current position. According to the United States Geological Survey, this is also when the Rocky Mountains started to form during the Laramide orogeny (mountain-building event). This process of uplifting and glacial erosion continued until about 55 to 35 million years ago. You can see the various rock layers in Colorado's many formations along the Front Range today.

Flora and Fauna

Colorado is home to a diverse mix of plants and animals thanks to a range of elevation, landscapes, and temperatures.

In the plains closer to the cities, there are more grasses. As you move up in elevation and precipitation, you'll see more variety: shrublands change into piñon-juniper forests, then ponderosa pine and Douglas fir–filled forests. Then there's lodgepole pines and aspens, spruce-firs and bristlecone pines—all with mountain grasslands, wetlands, and meadows throughout. Look for the state flower, the blue-and-white Columbine, at higher elevations, plus an assortment of wildflowers throughout the region: blue Front Range beardtongue, wispy mountain mahogany, classic black-eyed Susans, red wholeleaf Indian paintbrush, and aspen daisies, among others. Most wildflowers bloom from mid- to late spring until mid- to late summer, but some (such as the aspen daisy) peak from midsummer to mid-fall. You'll start to notice which flowers prefer sunny meadows and which prefer shaded creek beds.

Above it all sits the alpine tundra. Usually found at elevations above 11,000 feet, you'll quickly see why this region is called "above the treeline." The environment here is harsh—short, cool summers; long, cold winters with lots of wind and snow— and no trees grow at this elevation. Here, you'll find mostly grasses, mosses, lichens, and other small and fragile plants. Few animals call the alpine tundra home, but those that do include pika, yellow-bellied marmot, rosy finch, and white-tailed ptarmigan.

An abundance of animals live in the forests between the treeline and the plains (and in the water), so keep your eyes peeled for Steller's jays, golden eagles, red-tailed

The Colorado blue columbine (the state flower) is usually only found at higher elevations, but you might get lucky and spot one in lower elevations, like along the Evergreen Mountain Trail.

hawks, prairie falcons, mule deer, elk, moose, and foxes. At higher elevations, you may see mountain goats and Rocky Mountain bighorn sheep. Squirrels and cheeky chipmunks are widespread throughout the Front Range too, and may even come right up to you to beg for food, especially in Rocky Mountain National Park. As cute as they are, never feed wild animals, as they may learn to rely on humans instead of their natural instincts. It's also good practice to give the larger animals plenty of space, as some can be dangerous and will charge if you get too close. Animals you won't likely see—and you don't want to!—include mountain lions in rocky areas and black bears in the forests. Back on the plains, prairie dogs, mule and white-tailed deer, squirrels, and coyotes are plentiful.

Several snakes make their homes in the Front Range, and *almost* all of them are harmless. That being said, you'll often see signs at trailheads warning about rattlesnakes. The prairie rattlesnake is found up to elevations of 9,500 feet and prefers rocky canyons and open prairies. You are most likely to come across one sunning itself on a south-facing hillside or rock in the spring or fall. Therefore, it's essential to keep your

Deer are plentiful on many trails in the Front Range and beyond.

dog on a leash or under voice control and not allow them to sniff around under rock piles. Other snakes may mimic the rattle sound, but if you hear it, it is better to be safe than sorry and get out of the area or give the snake a wide berth. Never try to catch, kill, or move a rattlesnake.

Last but not least, don't forget to look in the crystal-clear lakes for brown, brook, rainbow, and cutthroat (Colorado River and Yellowstone) trout swimming around. The greenback cutthroat trout, Colorado's state fish, was once presumed to be extinct. It is still on the federal threatened species list, but ongoing efforts to reestablish the native population have been successful and the trout may be removed from the list entirely.

When viewing wildlife, use this rule of thumb from the Rocky Mountain National Park visitor guide: Make a thumbs-up and extend your arm all the way out. Close one eye and line your thumb up with the animal. If you can still see the animal behind your thumb, back away until your thumb completely covers the animal. Now you're at a safe distance!

Chipmunks have gotten very good at begging for a treat, like this little one who hung out inches away from me to eat something it found and then almost jumped in my lap to see if I had anything (I did not).

The waters in Rocky Mountain National Park are rich with trout.

Many trails close to the cities are accessible and clear in the winter.

Weather

While many think of Colorado as snowy and cold for much of the year, the opposite is actually true. We enjoy more than 300 days of sunshine annually, and even in the winter, temperatures are mostly moderate in the Front Range. Barring trail closures due to mud or snow, it's possible to hike many of the trails in this book year-round. Our snowiest months are March and April, but you can also count on a random snowstorm hitting in May.

Spring temperatures in the Front Range near the cities average about 60 to 70°F. Summers can be as warm as the mid-90s (or higher), though most of the summer months are in the mid-80s. The trails closer to the cities are beautiful in the morning or later in the day during the summer. Fall is a gorgeous time to experience these trails, too, as the temperatures cool down and the weather is more predictable. Winters are mostly mild and in the 40s.

> **Expect the temperature to drop about 4 to 5°F for every 1,000 feet of elevation gain. For this reason, always bring layers when hiking at higher elevations.**

As you get farther into the mountains, the snow tends to stick around until June—or even July if it's been a particularly snowy season. Summer is the best time to hit the higher elevations and Rocky Mountain National Park since the weather is cooler up there, but afternoon thunderstorms and the accompanying threat of lightning are common in the early months of the summer, so plan to hike early in the day.

Summer Storms

Afternoon thunderstorms are common in both Denver and the mountains in the early to midsummer. But it's not the rain that you need to worry about—it's the lightning. That's why we strongly recommend getting your hike in early in the summer and getting off a peak or away from an exposed area if a storm is rolling in.

But even with the best intentions, storms can build quickly and take you by surprise. If you find yourself stuck in a thunderstorm, here are a few tips:

- Don't try to run back to your car. Take shelter, ideally in a group of smaller, same-sized trees. Lightning storms don't usually last very long, so it's better to wait it out.
- Don't hang out under lone trees, in the open, or near standing water.
- Crouch with both feet firmly on the ground.
- Move away from anything metal, like a walking pole, backpack with a metal frame, etc.
- If you have a backpack (without a metal frame) or sleeping pad, stand on it for extra insulation in the event you get struck by lightning.
- Don't walk or huddle with your hiking partner(s). Stay 50 feet apart from each other.

Altitude Sickness

Even if you live in Colorado, altitude sickness can hit the hardiest among us. Acute mountain sickness (AMS) occurs when you move to a higher altitude too quickly and your body has difficulty adjusting to the lack of oxygen. AMS is the most common form of altitude sickness and can cause headaches, dizziness, irritability, nausea, vomiting, loss of appetite, fatigue, and shortness of breath. It's common to experience some level of fatigue, shortness of breath, and change in your appetite when hiking at altitude, but anything out of the ordinary could be moving into AMS. If you're experiencing more extreme symptoms or can't tell for sure, call it a day and head back down. It's not worth it!

Hydration, rest, and acclimation are key here. If you're coming from sea level, give yourself a few days to get used to being at elevation before attempting a hike, especially one of the trails at higher elevations.

Dogs can make fantastic hiking companions—just be sure to follow all rules and regulations around access.

Hiking with Dogs

If you are a dog person, you likely want to take your pup on fun adventures, and that includes hiking. But it's important to consider what is best for your dog's activity level and interests. Just as we have to get in shape, don't take your pup out for an early season 8-miler unless you've been keeping up their fitness over the winter.

It's also essential to know the regulations for where you're planning to go. Many areas require dogs to stay on leash not just for the safety of other hikers, but to prevent them from chasing wildlife or getting themselves in a dangerous situation. If the area does not require a dog to be on a leash, ensure your dog follows voice commands and always have your leash handy just in case. Some hikes, like those in Rocky Mountain National Park and some state parks, do not allow dogs on trails at all.

Always bring extra water for your four-legged hiking companion, and if the forecast is especially hot or cold, consider leaving them at home.

Always pick up after your dog. Many trailheads at least have a trash can, so use it!

Trail Etiquette

First and foremost, anyone who enjoys the outdoors should practice the seven Leave No Trace principles (learn more at lnt.org):

- Plan ahead and prepare.
- Travel and camp on durable surfaces.
- Dispose of waste properly (including the aforementioned dog poop).
- Leave what you find.
- Minimize campfire impacts (look up specific fire restrictions for your destination before you go).
- Respect wildlife (per Colorado Parks & Wildlife, it's illegal to harass or chase animals or birds).
- Be considerate of other visitors.

Many multiuse trails have signage to remind users about yielding.

Part of being considerate is knowing and following trail etiquette:

- Yield to uphill hikers if you're coming downhill.
- Hikers yield to horses, and mountain bikers yield to hikers and horses (though it's often easier for hikers to move out of the way of mountain bikers).
- Move off the trail if you're taking a break or a picture.
- If you're hiking with a group, don't take up the entire path, and move over so that others can pass you.
- Pack out what you pack in, even fruit litter like an apple core or banana peel.
- Don't play music—enjoy your company and the sounds of nature.
- If you need to relieve yourself, go at least 200 yards (about 70 steps) off the trail and away from a water source, and dig a 6- to 8-inch hole to go in if you need to defecate.

How to Use This Guide

With forty main hikes and eight additional bonus hikes, this guide has all the information you need to find your next Front Range adventure. Hikes range from 1.4 to 13 miles, with overall trail elevations ranging from 5,088 feet to one of the highest peaks in the country at 14,270 feet.

Each section begins with an **introduction to the region.** Hikes are split up by region based on the closest major city. Each hike begins with a short **summary** of the route's highlights and why it is included in this book. After the overview, you'll find the **at-a-glance specs,** aka the details you need to know to do the hike. The specs include:

Start: Where the trail begins, which is usually also where it ends.

Distance: The total distance and type of trail (out-and-back, lollipop, loop, figure eight). Some may include options to make the trail shorter or longer.

Difficulty: Hikes are designated as easy, moderate, or strenuous for the average hiker. Note that difficulty ratings can be subjective depending on your fitness, acclimation to altitude, etc. If you are coming from sea level and/or don't have much hiking experience, it may help to bump up the rating to give you an idea of what to expect. Either way, this is just a guideline and you may find the trail to be easier or more difficult.

Elevation gain: The total elevation change from the lowest point of the hike to the highest.

Hiking time: Everyone is different, so this number is a median range considering that most hikers can cover, on average, about 2.5 to 3.5 miles an hour.

Trail surface: This gives you an idea of what type of path you'll be walking on.

Seasons/schedule: The best time of year for the hike and when the trail is open to the public. Note that any trail closer to town that simply says "year-round" implies there isn't heavy snow on the ground, although many of these trails are still accessible with spikes even when there has been a recent snow.

Fees and permits: Any fees associated with a hike will be listed here, including trail access or parking fees, park entrance fees, etc.

Other trail users: Who to watch out for while hiking along the trail (mountain bikers, equestrians, cross-country skiers, etc.).

Canine compatibility: Whether or not dogs are allowed on the trail and under what conditions.

Land status: Whether the trail is in a state park, national park, wilderness area, county open space, etc.

Trail contact: The direct contact information for the local land manager in charge of the trails in the selected hike so that you can call ahead for trail updates; report problems with trail erosion, damage, or misuse; or find out how you can help maintain the trails.

The view of Golden from the Mount Galbraith Loop.

Maps: Official maps that you may want to use to supplement the maps in this guidebook.

Nearest town: The nearest substantial town with at least a gas station and some supplies.

Cell service: Service may vary by carrier, but this will give you a general idea of what you can expect while out on the trail.

Special considerations: Anything you need to know about the specific trail, such as no water, no shade, etc.

After the specs, there is a section for **Finding the trailhead.** Here you'll find directions from the closest major city (Fort Collins, Denver, Colorado Springs) to the trailhead parking area. This section will include the GPS coordinates for the start point.

Now for **The Hike.** This section offers a description of the trail plus interesting information about the area's history and what you might see and can expect along the way. It goes more in-depth than the specs, and is a direct result of the author's experience on the trail.

Miles and Directions break down the turns, intersections, trail changes, and any viewpoints or notable landmarks. After this section, some trails have **Additional Route Options** if you'd like to shorten or lengthen the hike.

There will also be bonus hikes at the end of each region (except Rocky Mountain National Park—just about every hike there could qualify as a bonus hike!). These hikes didn't make the main list but are still worth checking out and/or are local favorites.

How to Use the Maps

The overview map in the front of the guide shows all of the hikes across the Front Range in one place. Each route will also have its own, more detailed map that shows roads, points of interest, water features, landmarks, the main trail, and other trails. The main trail will be highlighted and have directional arrows so that you know which way to go.

Trail Finder

Best Hikes for Families
- 2 Devil's Backbone Loop
- 7 Davidson Mesa Open Space
- 17 Flatirons Vista Trail
- 24 Peaks to Plains Trail—Gateway Trailhead
- 36 Paint Mines Interpretive Park
- 38 Susan G. Bretag and Palmer Loop
- 40 Fountain Creek Nature Trail
- B Poudre River Trail

Best Hikes for Dogs
- 7 Davidson Mesa Open Space
- 16 Rattlesnake Gulch—Eldorado Canyon State Park
- 17 Flatirons Vista Trail
- 19 Raccoon Trail—Golden Gate Canyon State Park
- 24 Peaks to Plains Trail—Gateway Trailhead
- E O'Fallon Park Loop

Best Hikes for Water Features
- 3 Dream and Emerald Lakes—Rocky Mountain National Park
- 4 Lake Haiyaha Loop—Rocky Mountain National Park
- 5 Ouzel Falls via Wild Basin Trail—Rocky Mountain National Park
- 6 Finch Lake via Allenspark Trail—Rocky Mountain National Park
- 14 Ceran St. Vrain Trail to Miller Rock
- 20 Beaver Brook and Chavez Trail Loop
- 29 St. Mary's Glacier and James Peak

Best Hikes if You Want to Stay Close to Town
- 1 Horsetooth Falls Loop
- 2 Devil's Backbone Loop
- 9 Royal Arch Trail
- 22 Dakota Ridge Trail
- 24 Peaks to Plains Trail—Gateway Trailhead
- 38 Susan G. Bretag and Palmer Loop
- 40 Fountain Creek Nature Trail

Best Hikes to Get Your Heart Pumping

- 3 Dream and Emerald Lakes—Rocky Mountain National Park
- 4 Lake Haiyaha Loop—Rocky Mountain National Park
- 9 Royal Arch Trail
- 15 Crater Lakes via South Boulder Creek Trail
- 20 Beaver Brook and Chavez Trail Loop
- 22 Dakota Ridge Trail
- 30 Grays and Torreys Peaks

Best Hikes for Mountain Views

- 14 Ceran St. Vrain Trail to Miller Rock
- 16 Rattlesnake Gulch—Eldorado Canyon State Park
- 28 Staunton Ranch, Old Mill, and Border Line Trails—Staunton State Park
- 29 St. Mary's Glacier and James Peak
- 30 Grays and Torreys Peaks
- 31 South Park 600 Trail to Square Top Lakes
- 35 Devil's Head Lookout Trail

Map Legend

Transportation

≡(25)≡ Interstate Highway

≡(36)≡ US Highway

≡(119)≡ State Highway

≡(93)≡ Local/County/Forest Road

= = = = Gravel Road

= = = = Unpaved Road

------ Featured Trail

------ Trail

+—+—+ Railroad

Water Features

◯ Body of Water

〰 River/Creek

〰 Intermittent Creek

≋ Waterfall

⊶ Spring

Land Management

▭ National Park/
Wilderness

▭ State/Local/
Open Space Park

Symbols

♿ Accessible Trail

🚾 Bench

⏝ Bridge

▲ Campground

⊞ Cliff

🅿 Parking

▲ Peak/Summit

🔥 Picnic Area

■ Point of Interest/Structure

🏠 Ranger Station

🚻 Restroom

|||||| Steps

🗼 Tower

○ Town

① Trailhead

🏞 Viewpoint/Overlook

❓ Visitor Center/Information Center

Fort Collins Area

Fort Collins, known as FoCo to locals, sits in northern Colorado 40 miles south of the Wyoming border. For thousands of years, Indigenous people called Larimer County home, including the Ute, Arapaho, Cheyenne, Lakota, Apache, and Comanche, according to Fort Collins History Connection. In the 1840s, white settlers and trappers started crossing the land along the Oregon Trail, introducing contagious diseases and disrupting traditional grazing lands. In the 1850s and '60s treaties were introduced, eventually resulting in the Indigenous people being pushed to reservations in other states.

The nearby town of LaPorte was originally named Camp Collins on July 22, 1862, by soldiers from the Ninth Kansas Cavalry. The post was established to protect the Cherokee Trail and Overland Stage Line, but was wiped out after a devastating flood in June 1864. The place that is now known as Fort Collins was recommended as a prime spot to move the operations, and on August 20, 1864, Lieutenant Colonel William O. Collins officially designated this site as the new military reservation.

Today, Fort Collins is known for Colorado State University, more than twenty craft breweries (including the fourth-largest craft brewer in the country, New Belgium Brewing Company), and outdoor recreation. With more than fifty parks, miles of walking and biking trails, the Cache La Poudre River running through the northern part of the city, and easy access to the popular Horsetooth Reservoir, there are plenty of ways to enjoy the outdoors here. Legend has it that the river was named Cache La Poudre by French-Canadian trappers who got stuck in the area during a terrible snowstorm in the 1800s. After camping by the waterway and waiting out the storm, they buried large amounts of gunpowder (*poudre*) in hidden places (*cache*) along the river to lighten their wagons and continue their journey.

The prickly poppy is found from the plains to the foothills and blooms from March through October.

1 Horsetooth Falls Loop

Located just west of the popular Horsetooth Reservoir, this hike leads to a seasonal waterfall that is best in the late spring. You'll trek through the open hillside, a riparian corridor along Spring Creek, and a rolling meadow.

Start: Horsetooth Mountain Trailhead at Horsetooth Mountain Open Space
Distance: 3.4-mile lollipop
Difficulty: Moderate
Elevation gain: 580 feet
Hiking time: 1.5–2 hours
Trail surface: Rocky
Seasons/schedule: Year-round; best late spring to early summer for the waterfall. The park is closed from 11 p.m. to 4 a.m. daily.
Fees and permits: Daily entrance fee or annual entrance permit required
Other trail users: None
Canine compatibility: Dogs allowed on leash

Land status: Larimer County Parks and Open Space
Trail contact: Larimer County Department of Natural Resources; (970) 619-4570; www.larimer.gov/naturalresources
Maps: Horsetooth Mountain Open Space
Nearest town: Fort Collins
Cell service: Spotty
Special considerations: This trail is subject to closure due to weather or muddy conditions. The parking lot fills up quickly on summer weekends, so it is recommended to arrive before 9 a.m. or after 3 p.m.

Finding the trailhead: Starting at South College Avenue (US 287) and West Mulberry Street in Fort Collins, go west on West Mulberry for 2 miles. Turn left onto South Taft Hill Road and continue for 3.5 miles. Go right on West CR 38E for 6.5 miles and turn right into the Horsetooth Mountain Open Space parking lot. GPS: N40 31.44' / W105 10.87'

The Hike

From the parking lot, there are two trails: go to the northern option and follow the sign for the Horsetooth Rock Trail and Horsetooth Falls Trail. The Horsetooth Falls Trail is designated by a purple circle with a white arrow. When you get to the intersection of the two trails, go right toward an open hillside that overlooks a gulch. (Scan the steep hillside across the gulch for mule deer munching on the grass!) From here, the trail drops down. You'll eventually cross a bridge over Spring Creek. A steep climb up rock steps along a ponderosa pine–lined path leads to the junction with

> Horsetooth Rock, reaching 7,256 feet above sea level, is a famous landmark in the area. Local legend says Horsetooth Rock is the remains of an evil giant's heart, cut in two places by the mighty Chief Maunamoku (also known as Great Buffalo) to protect his people and their hunting grounds. After the chief killed the giant, the heart turned to stone.

The flow of the falls varies by season.

The final descent back to the trailhead offers sweeping views of the surrounding foothills.

the Spring Creek Trail at 1.2 miles. Go left on the Horsetooth Falls Trail to the falls, which are also on your left.

Depending on the season, the waterfall will be either a rushing cascade or a slight trickle, but there is a bench nearby and this makes for a nice place for a break to listen to the sounds of the water. Go back the way you came on the Horsetooth Falls Trail until you return to the junction with the Spring Creek Trail; turn left and head north to continue your rocky climb. After it levels out, you'll reach the Soderberg Trail and cross Spring Creek again. Here, wildflowers grow along the water and tall rocks surround you—another great spot to stop for a moment and take it all in.

Turn left to head south on the Soderberg Trail and climb through a stand of ponderosas. There will be an open meadow on your left with red rocks in the distance—a beautiful sight! The trail will widen and start a gradual climb, connecting with the Horsetooth Rock Trail and leading to fantastic views before descending back down to the parking lot.

Miles and Directions

0.0 Start at the parking lot at the trailhead with the sign for the Horsetooth Rock Trail and Horsetooth Falls Trail.

Follow the purple signs to stay on the Horsetooth Falls Loop.

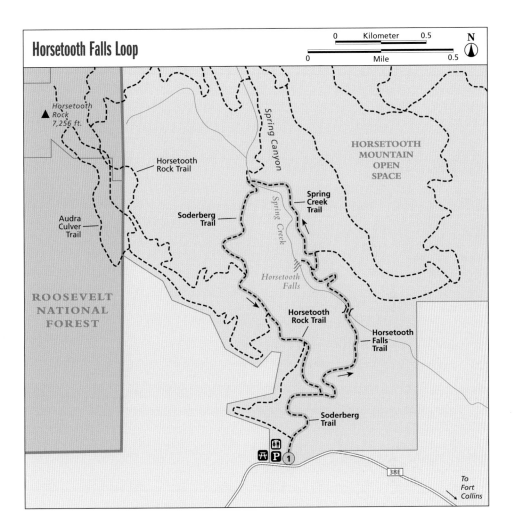

Horsetooth Falls Loop

0 Kilometer **0.5**

0 Mile **0.5**

N

Horsetooth Rock 7,256 ft.

Horsetooth Rock Trail

Spring Canyon

HORSETOOTH MOUNTAIN OPEN SPACE

Spring Creek Trail

Soderberg Trail

Spring Creek

Audra Culver Trail

Horsetooth Falls

ROOSEVELT NATIONAL FOREST

Horsetooth Rock Trail

Horsetooth Falls Trail

Soderberg Trail

38E

To Fort Collins

0.4 Go right on the Horsetooth Falls Trail.

1.2 Come to junction with the Spring Creek Trail; go left.

1.3 Arrive at Horsetooth Falls.

1.4 Arrive back at the junction with the Spring Creek Trail; go left.

1.8 Reach a junction with the Soderberg Trail; go left.

2.2 Continue straight onto the Horsetooth Rock Trail.

2.4 Continue straight to stay on the Horsetooth Rock Trail.

2.6 Continue straight to stay on the Horsetooth Rock Trail.

2.8 Come to the junction with the Horsetooth Falls Trail; go right to return to the parking lot.

3.4 Arrive back at the trailhead.

The scenery changes every season, making many of these hikes worth a repeat.

Additional Route Options

To visit the namesake Horsetooth Rock, take a right at 2.2 miles and follow the trail to the top at 7,256 feet. This will add about 3 miles to your trip.

2 Devil's Backbone Loop

This is one of several hikes in this book that is a must for geology buffs and bird-watchers. See this unique hogback formation up close, peek through The Keyhole, and keep an eye out for the birds that make their homes within the rocks.

Start: Devil's Backbone Trailhead
Distance: 4.4-mile double loop
Difficulty: Easy
Elevation gain: 480 feet
Hiking time: 1.5-2 hours
Trail surface: Dirt and rocks
Seasons/schedule: Year-round; best in the spring and fall. The open space is open from sunrise to sunset.
Fees and permits: Daily entrance fee or annual entrance permit required
Other trail users: The Wild Loop is hiking only; mountain bikers are allowed on the Hunter Loop.
Canine compatibility: Dogs allowed on leash

Land status: Larimer County Parks and Open Space
Trail contact: Larimer County Department of Natural Resources; (970) 619-4570; www .larimer.gov/naturalresources
Maps: Devil's Backbone Open Space
Nearest town: Loveland
Cell service: Good
Special considerations: This trail is subject to closure due to weather or muddy conditions. The parking lot can get full on weekends, so it's recommended to arrive early. There is no other parking here besides the designated lot. Always stay on designated trails—do not climb on the rocks. The trail is exposed with no tree cover except the first/last 0.1 mile.

Finding the trailhead: Starting at South College Avenue (US 287) and West Mulberry Street in Fort Collins, go south on South College for 1 mile. Turn right onto West Prospect Road for 2 miles, then turn left onto South Taft Hill Road for 8 miles. Continue onto Wilson Avenue for 3.1 miles, then turn right onto West Eisenhower Boulevard (US 34) for 2.1 miles. Turn right onto Hidden Valley Drive for 0.3 mile and turn left into the Devil's Backbone Open Space parking lot. GPS: N40 24.70' / W105 19.18'

The Hike

Devil's Backbone is a special landmark in Larimer County. Not only because of the striking ridgeline, but also because it was also once home to prehistoric animals, including an elephant with 5-foot-long tusks. After becoming the county's first designated open space in 1999, the area has since grown to cover more than 3,000 acres and 17.25 miles of trail that connect to Rimrock Open Space and Horsetooth Mountain Open Space.

The hike starts in the parking lot near the restrooms (the northern part of the parking lot). Follow the trail past a picnic area (the picnic area will be on your left), cross the

Before the region was called Devil's Backbone, it had several other names, including Bears' Cathedral.

On this hike, walk along the unique Devil's Backbone Formation, rising 200-plus feet toward the sky.

footbridge, and bear left to go up the steps to the start of the Wild Loop. This interpretive trail is open to foot traffic only. You'll see a trail down to your right through the grass—that's the Hidden Valley Trail and it's only open to bikers and runners. For this hike, you'll stay closer to the rock formation.

When you get to the split of the Wild Loop around 0.4 mile, continue straight to hit the main sights on the way back. At 1.2 miles you can turn left to continue around the loop for a 2.5-mile hike, but I highly recommend continuing on the Hunter Loop for an amazing view of the backbone. Wildflowers, like the prickly poppy with its papery thin petals and bright yellow center, line the path.

You may encounter mountain bikers as you work your way up the 0.4-mile climb to Hunter Loop. While you catch your breath, take a minute to look back at the Devil's Backbone for a bird's-eye view. After following the loop around clockwise, come back down the way you came to finish the Wild Loop.

Besides the opportunity to see the hogback formation up close, there are two notable sights along this section of the loop: The Keyhole and a scenic view of the mountains to the west. At 3.5 miles, you'll see a sign and spur trail going west up to the feature. Cliff swallows, ravens, great horned owls, and red-tailed hawks live among

The Keyhole offers views of a popular 14er, Longs Peak.

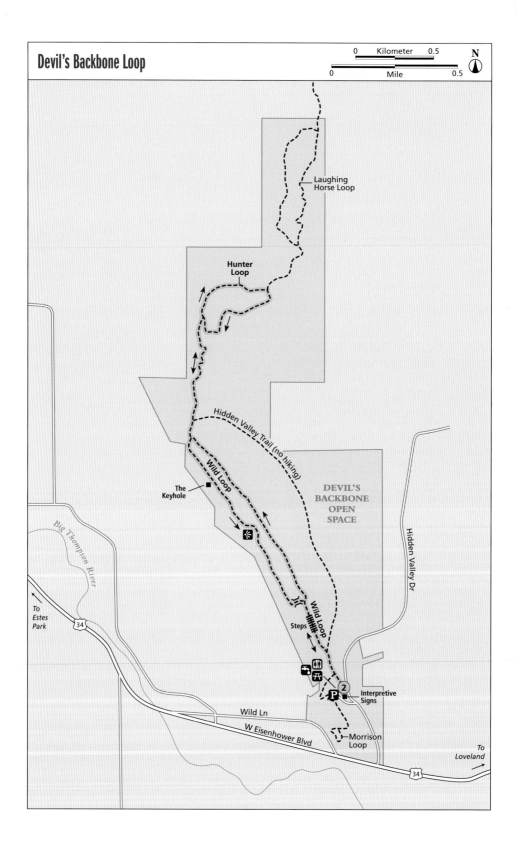

The trail is rich with wildflowers during the summer. Look for the prickly-pear cactus, bush sunflower, copper mallow, fringed sage, western wallflower, and others along the way. The rare Bell's twinpod can also be found here among the shale and sandstone. It's only found in outcrops in Larimer, Boulder, and Douglas Counties in May and June.

the rocks up here. From both The Keyhole and the viewpoint, you'll see the neighborhood below the ridge, and in the distance, a cluster of several notable peaks rising above the rest: Mount Meeker (13,811 feet) to the left, then Longs Peak (14,251 feet) rising up in the middle, Mount Lady Washington (13,281 feet) to the right of that, and Storm Peak (13,326 feet). The smaller mountains directly in front of Mount Meeker and Longs Peak are the 11,428-foot Twin Sisters.

A little farther south at 3.8 miles is the viewpoint. When you get there, the trail you'll see on your left is neighborhood access only, so return to the Wild Loop and finish the way you came. Depending on the time of day of your hike, there are sometimes mule deer grazing in the grassy area near the Hidden Valley Trail.

Miles and Directions

0.0   Start at the northern part of the parking lot.

0.3   Cross a footbridge

0.4   Stay right on the Wild Loop.

1.2   Continue straight to stay on the lower section of the Wild Loop.

1.3   Continue straight to stay on the lower section of the Wild Loop.

2.1   Continue straight at the intersection with the Laughing Horse Loop trail to stay on the Hunter Loop.

2.6   Turn left to go back down to the Wild Loop.

3.3   Bear right onto the Wild Loop.

3.5   Arrive at The Keyhole.

3.8   Arrive at the viewpoint.

4.1   Turn right to return to the parking lot.

4.4   Arrive back at the parking lot.

Additional Route Options

From the parking lot, the Wild Loop by itself is a 2.5-mile hike. In addition to the Hunter Loop route described here, there is also the option to add the Laughing Horse Loop for an additional 1.5 miles. For even more mileage, you could add a third loop. From the Laughing Horse Loop, take the Blue Sky Trail for 1.4 miles to the Indian Summer Trail, a 2.8-mile loop. The Blue Sky Trail also connects to Coyote Ridge Natural Area and Horsetooth Mountain Open Space. Pick up a map at the Devil's Backbone Trailhead for more details.

Bonus Hikes at a Glance

A. Lory State Park

Lory State Park is west of Fort Collins and Horsetooth Reservoir, offering twenty-eight trails ranging in distance and difficulty. Trails run through valleys and gulches and across hillsides, but the grade rarely exceeds 12 percent and most trails are hiking only, which means there are options for hikers of all levels and abilities. One of the most popular options at the park is the 4.5-mile Arthur's Rock to Howard Loop Trail. Considered a moderate hike, the route climbs up to 6,780-foot Arthur's Rock for expansive views of Horsetooth Reservoir and beyond. Start at the trailhead and expect open meadows filled with wildflowers, ponderosas, cottonwoods, and more natural beauty on this trail. Dogs are allowed, on leash.

Finding the trailhead: Starting at South College Avenue (US 287) and West Mulberry Street in Fort Collins, go west on West Mulberry for 3 miles. Turn right onto South Overland Trail for 2.8 miles, then turn left onto Bingham Hill Road for 1.9 miles. Turn left onto CR 23 and continue for 1.2 miles. Turn right onto Lodgepole Drive for 1.6 miles, then turn left to stay on Lodgepole Drive for 2.2 miles to the trailhead at the end of the road. GPS: N40 33.87' / W105 10.53'

The Cache de Poudre River originates in Rocky Mountain National Park and flows down to meet the South Platte River east of Greeley.

B. Poudre River Trail

If you're looking for a family-friendly option for all ages, this is it. The paved walking and bike path follows the Cache de Poudre River corridor starting at Island Grove Regional Park in Greeley and ending 21 miles later at CO 392 in Windsor, where it connects to River Bluffs Open Space. The route's starting point, Island Grove, was named after the stand of cottonwood trees growing here. It was also once a burial site for the Arapahoe, Cheyenne, and Sioux, as well as settlers. Signature Bluffs Natural Area is a large river habitat with a pond, cottonwood stands, cattails, and meadows, and the Kodak Watchable Wildlife Area is a great place to spot wild turkeys, eagles, hawks, and waterfowl. Dogs are allowed on leash and much of the property around the trail is private, so stay on the designated trail at all times. Learn more about the trail and trailheads at www.poudretrail.org.

Rocky Mountain National Park

While we know there were people inhabiting the landscape now known as Rocky Mountain National Park (RMNP) some 11,000 years ago, we still know very little about the early people here, according to the National Park Service (NPS). We do know that the Utes lived in the area until the late 1700s, and then the US government acquired

The Wild Basin Trail follows North St. Vrain Creek through the forest and passes Copeland Falls and Calypso Cascades en route to the grand finale.

the land as part of the Louisiana Purchase in 1803. Early settlers mostly avoided the rugged landscape until the Pikes Peak Gold Rush of 1859.

The conservation and preservation movement started picking up steam in 1900, and in 1909 naturalist, nature guide, and lodge owner Enos Mills became an advocate for protecting the area as a national park. On January 26, 1915, President Woodrow Wilson signed the Rocky Mountain National Park Act and it became the ninth national park in the country (but second in Colorado, behind Mesa Verde National Park in 1906).

Since then, RMNP has grown to become the fourth-most-visited park in the United States, leading the NPS to institute a reservation system for admission. It's difficult to have any kind of "best hikes" book in Colorado without including at least a few from RMNP, so this list represents my best effort to include two of the most iconic (and popular) hikes, plus two others that are incredible in their own right, but without as much foot traffic.

Weather in Rocky Mountain National Park is notoriously fickle, so check the radar in advance and plan for anything. You can usually avoid afternoon storms by getting to the trailhead early—and you skip a lot of the tourist traffic this way too!

3 Dream and Emerald Lakes Trail

This trail is in the most popular area of the park, the Bear Lake Corridor. Dream and Emerald Lakes are a little easier of a hike than the trek to Lake Haiyaha, and are well worth dealing with the logistics.

Start: Bear Lake Trailhead
Distance: 3.6 miles out and back
Difficulty: Easy
Elevation gain: 744 feet
Hiking time: 1.5–2 hours
Trail surface: Paved in the beginning and then dirt
Seasons/schedule: Summer through fall. The park is open 24/7, weather permitting.
Fees and permits: Daily entrance fee or America the Beautiful annual pass. Between May 26 and October 22, you'll also need a Park Access Plus Timed Entry Permit (specific for Bear Lake Corridor), available at recreation.gov.
Other trail users: None
Canine compatibility: No dogs allowed
Land status: Rocky Mountain National Park
Trail contact: Rocky Mountain National Park; (970) 586-1206; www.nps.gov/romo

Maps: USGS Rocky Mountain National Park
Nearest town: Estes Park
Cell service: None
Special considerations: Have your timed reservation ready when you pull up to the entrance booth. Cell service may be limited, so we suggest opening the app or email while in Estes Park (or print your reservation ahead of time). There is limited parking at the trailhead. If the trailhead is full, a complimentary shuttle is available. This lot is 5 miles along Bear Lake Road on your right. Another option is to reserve a spot on the hiker shuttle from the Estes Park Visitor Center (also available on recreation .gov). You will still need a valid park entrance fee or America the Beautiful pass. Spots are limited on the shuttles as well, so plan accordingly. Timed reservations often sell out well in advance for peak periods.

Finding the trailhead: From the Beaver Meadows entrance to the national park, take US 36 a short distance west to Bear Lake Road. Turn left and drive 9 miles to the road's end at the Bear Lake parking lot. GPS: N40 18.72' / W105 38.75'

The Hike

It's easy to see why Dream Lake is one of the most popular hikes in the national park—not only is it a short trek that is accessible to most everyone, but it also exemplifies the beauty of the area. A steady climb through aspen groves and ponderosa pines leads first to the lily-pad-covered Nymph Lake just 0.5 mile in, which is a great spot for a break if you need one. The lake was named after the original name of the pond lilies here, *Nymphaea polysepala* (the flower has since been renamed *Nuphar polysepala*).

Continue on—taking in the views at 0.8 mile—and then at the 1-mile mark, you'll come to an intersection with the trail to Lake Haiyaha. Follow the sign and turn right to Dream Lake. The calm, clear waters of Dream Lake reflect the false summit of Hallett Peak and the spires of Flattop Mountain. Many visitors choose to

Crystal-clear Dream Lake is just 1.1 miles from the trailhead.

turn around here, but it's only another 0.7 mile to Emerald Lake, and it's worth the extra distance.

As you round the right side of the lake to continue on the trail, it's easy to get distracted by the view, but be sure to look into the water for greenback cutthroat trout, Colorado's state fish. Once presumed to be extinct, the fish is still on the federal threatened species list, but ongoing efforts to reestablish the native population in places like Rocky Mountain National Park have been successful and the trout may be removed from the list entirely. Dream and Emerald Lakes are catch-and-release fishing only.

Emerald Lake is a true gem (pun intended). It's postcard-perfect (or Instagram-worthy, whichever you prefer): the beautiful green-jeweled color of the water, the dark green of the trees, and the mix of gray rocks with a few patches of snow mixed in here and there is a sight to behold. You can hear a waterfall of runoff on the opposite side, and you get a closer view of Hallett and Flattop.

Miles and Directions

0.0 Start at the Bear Lake Trailhead. The trail to Dream and Emerald Lakes will be at the west end of the parking lot. Straight ahead is Bear Lake, so you'll go south to start this route (there are signs and rangers available if you need help).

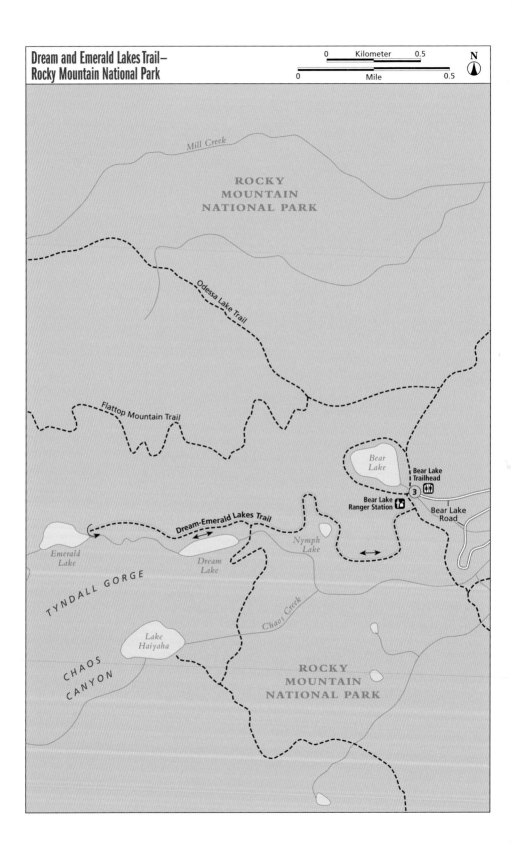

Dream and Emerald Lakes Trail–
Rocky Mountain National Park

0   Kilometer   0.5

0   Mile   0.5

N

Mill Creek

ROCKY
MOUNTAIN
NATIONAL PARK

Odessa Lake Trail

Flattop Mountain Trail

Bear
Lake

Bear Lake
Trailhead

3

Bear Lake
Ranger Station

Bear Lake
Road

Dream-Emerald Lakes Trail

Emerald
Lake

Dream
Lake

Nymph
Lake

TYNDALL GORGE

Chaos Creek

Lake
Haiyaha

CHAOS
CANYON

ROCKY
MOUNTAIN
NATIONAL PARK

Emerald Lake is worth the extra 0.7-mile trek.

0.5 Arrive at Nymph Lake. Continue around the right side of the lake.

1.0 Come to an intersection with the trail to Lake Haiyaha. Turn right (follow the sign) to Dream Lake.

1.1 Arrive at Dream Lake.

1.8 Arrive at Emerald Lake. Return the way you came.

3.6 Arrive back at the trailhead.

Additional Route Options

There is another lake on this route if you want to check off one more: Bear Lake. It's back at the trailhead and there's an easy paved walking path around it.

Along this hike, you're very likely to encounter an intrepid chipmunk or two. They will come right up to you, begging for a treat. While many think it's cute (and it is, to be honest), don't feed the wildlife. Human food isn't healthy for them—not even a little peanut—and it can lead to animals becoming dependent on snacks and starving when tourist season is over, or becoming aggressive and breaking into your bag/tent to get food. Be sure to clean up after stopping for a snack on the trail.

4 Lake Haiyaha Loop

Lake Haiyaha is a special place. The water is an incredible shade of blue that makes you wonder if it's really that color or if everyone has turned up the contrast in the editing process. I can confirm that yes, it is really that color. And this particular lake is more accessible than many of the higher alpine lakes across the state. As an added bonus, the loop stops by the 30-foot Alberta Falls on the way back.

Start: Bear Lake Trailhead
Distance: 5.2-mile loop
Difficulty: Moderate
Elevation gain: 846 feet
Hiking time: 3-4 hours
Trail surface: Paved in the beginning and then dirt
Seasons/schedule: Summer through fall. The park is open 24/7, weather permitting.
Fees and permits: Daily entrance fee or America the Beautiful annual pass. Between May 26 and October 22, you'll also need a Park Access Plus Timed Entry Permit (specific for Bear Lake Corridor), available at recreation.gov.
Other trail users: None
Canine compatibility: No dogs allowed
Land status: Rocky Mountain National Park
Trail contact: Rocky Mountain National Park; (970) 586-1206; www.nps.gov/romo

Maps: USGS Rocky Mountain National Park
Nearest town: Estes Park
Cell service: None
Special considerations: Have your timed reservation ready when you pull up to the entrance booth. Internet may be limited, so we suggest opening the app or email while in Estes Park. There is limited parking at the trailhead. If the trailhead is full, a complimentary shuttle is available at the lot that is 5 miles from the checkpoint on Bear Lake Road, on your right. Another option is to reserve a spot on the hiker shuttle from the Estes Park Visitor Center (also available on recreation .gov). You will still need a valid park entrance fee or America the Beautiful pass. Spots are limited on the shuttles as well, so plan accordingly. Timed reservations often sell out well in advance for peak periods.

Finding the trailhead: From the Beaver Meadows entrance to the national park, take US 36 a short distance west to Bear Lake Road. Turn left and drive 9 miles to the road's end at the Bear Lake parking lot. GPS: N40 18.72' / W105 38.75'

The Hike

The hike to Lake Haiyaha is slightly more strenuous than the trek to Dream and Emerald Lakes, which means a little less foot traffic. Once you get to the lake, there is some boulder scrambling involved to get to the water itself. A steady climb through aspen groves and ponderosa pines leads first to the lily-pad–covered Nymph Lake just 0.5 mile in, which is a great spot for a break. The lake was named after the original name of the pond lilies here, *Nymphaea polysepala* (the flower has since been renamed *Nuphar polysepala*).

Nymph Lake is the first lake you'll come to—it's the one covered in pond lilies.

Continue on—taking in the views at 0.8 mile—and then at the 1-mile mark, you'll come to an intersection with the trail to Lake Haiyaha. You can take a 0.1-mile detour to the right to Dream Lake if you'd like, or follow the sign and continue straight. The trail climbs up through the subalpine forest, winding around and opening up for views of Longs Peak and Glacier Gorge.

As you head back into the forest, you'll come to an intersection with the trail for Loch Vale and Glacier Gorge at 1.9 miles. Stay to the right and continue straight until you run into a massive pile of boulders. Welcome to Chaos Canyon. The frosty blue Lake Haiyaha sits on the other side of those boulders. Many people find it an easier scramble to go straight on or slightly to the left, but if you are a tad more adventurous and make your way around to the right/east side of the lake, you'll have fantastic views with few to no other people in your shot. If you're wondering why so few alpine lakes have this frosty blue color, it's from something called glacial flour. The pressure of the glacier turns rocks into a fine dust and when the glacier melts, it takes the dust with it. When the sunlight reflects off the glacial flour, it results in a gorgeous blue color.

On your way back, continue your loop by taking the turn right at the Loch Vale and Glacier Gorge intersection. In just over 4 miles, you'll see the 30-foot Alberta

The name Haiyaha means "rock," "lake of many rocks," or "big rocks," depending on the translation, and there is a bit of scrambling at the end to get to the view you see here.

Falls tumbling into Glacier Creek. The waterfall was named after Alberta Sprague, who, along with her husband, was one of the first settlers in Estes Park. This back part of the loop has some aspens mixed in, making it a nice hike for fall colors. At 0.8 mile farther, bear left at the junction to go back to the parking lot. There's one more junction at 5 miles—continue straight to get back to the trailhead/parking lot.

Miles and Directions

0.0   Start at the Bear Lake Trailhead. The trail will be at the west end of the parking lot. Straight ahead is Bear Lake, so you'll go south to start this route (there are signs and rangers available if you need help).

0.5   Arrive at Nymph Lake. Continue around the right side of the lake.

1.0   Come to an intersection with the Dream and Emerald Lakes Trail. Go straight.

1.9   Come to an intersection with the trail to Loch Vale and Glacier Gorge. Stay to the right and continue straight on the trail to Lake Haiyaha.

2.1   Arrive at Lake Haiyaha.

2.3   Arrive back at the intersection with the trail to Loch Vale and Glacier Gorge. Go right to continue on Haiyaha Trail toward the Glacier Gorge Trail.

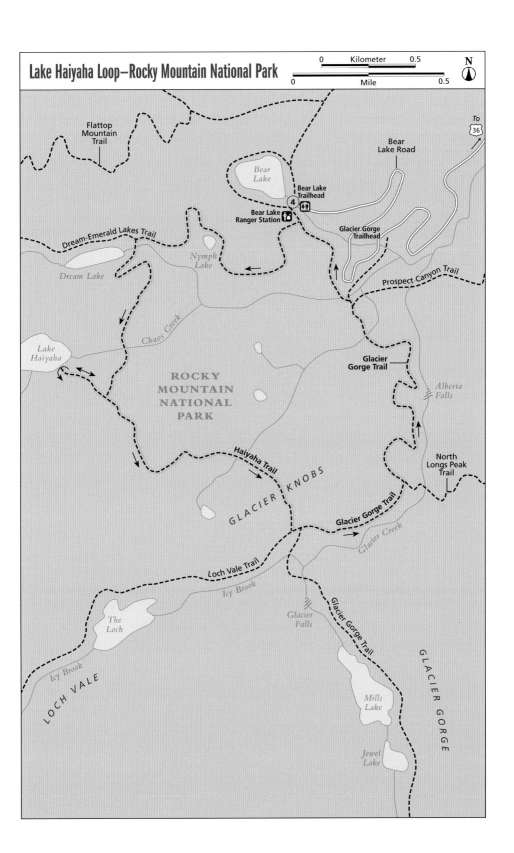

Lake Haiyaha Loop–Rocky Mountain National Park

Kilometer
0 0.5

Mile
0 0.5

N

Flattop
Mountain
Trail

Bear
Lake

Bear Lake
Trailhead

Bear Lake Road

To
36

Bear Lake
Ranger Station

4

Glacier Gorge
Trailhead

Dream-Emerald Lakes Trail

Nymph
Lake

Dream Lake

Prospect Canyon Trail

Chaos Creek

Lake
Haiyaha

ROCKY
MOUNTAIN
NATIONAL
PARK

Glacier
Gorge Trail

Alberta
Falls

Haiyaha Trail

GLACIER KNOBS

North
Longs Peak
Trail

Glacier Gorge Trail

Glacier Creek

Loch Vale Trail

Icy Brook

Glacier
Falls

Glacier Gorge Trail

The
Loch

Icy Brook

LOCH VALE

GLACIER GORGE

Mills
Lake

Jewel
Lake

You may feel a little more winded than usual when hiking in Rocky Mountain National Park and that's to be expected—for this hike, the trailhead starts at 9,475 feet and the high point is 10,240 feet. It's common to be a little more fatigued and have a mild headache and/or nausea, but if you vomit, feel dizzy, or symptoms continue to get worse, go back down to a lower elevation. Altitude sickness is not something you want to test. You can help prevent altitude sickness by staying hydrated and getting plenty of rest.

3.3 Come to a three-way junction with the Loch Vale Trail; turn left. Shortly after is the Glacier Gorge Trail; stay straight.

3.7 Stay straight to continue on the Glacier Gorge Trail. It may look like a shortcut, but the North Longs Peak Trail is not where you want to go.

4.1 Arrive at Alberta Falls.

4.8 At the trail junction, veer left to go back to the Bear Lake Trailhead/parking lot.

5.0 Continue straight toward trailhead/parking lot.

5.2 Arrive back at the trailhead/parking lot.

Additional Route Options

There is another lake on this route if you want to check off one more: Bear Lake. It's back at the trailhead and there's an easy paved walking path around it. If you get to Lake Haiyaha and want to take a faster route back, return the way you came to shave about a mile off your hike.

5 Ouzel Falls via Wild Basin Trail

If you're a fan of water features, this hike will quickly become one of your favorites. There are three waterfalls and you follow a whitewater stream the entire way. It's a gorgeous hike that isn't terribly difficult either, and it's in a less congested area of the park.

Start: Wild Basin Trailhead
Distance: 5.4 miles out and back
Difficulty: Moderately easy
Elevation gain: 984 feet
Hiking time: 2–3 hours
Trail surface: Dirt and rock
Seasons/schedule: Summer through fall. The park is open 24/7, weather permitting.
Fees and permits: Daily entrance fee or America the Beautiful annual pass. Between May 26 and October 22, you'll also need a Park Access Timed Entry Permit, available at recreation.gov.
Other trail users: None
Canine compatibility: No dogs allowed
Land status: Rocky Mountain National Park
Trail contact: Rocky Mountain National Park; (970) 586-1206; www.nps.gov/romo
Maps: USGS Allenspark
Nearest town: Allenspark

Cell service: None
Special considerations: Have your timed reservation ready when you pull up to the entrance booth. Internet may be limited, so we suggest opening the app or email while in Lyons (internet can be iffy all the way through Allenspark). Timed reservations often sell out well in advance for peak periods, but aren't required for this section of the park if you arrive before 9 a.m. or after 2 p.m. (The timing of the reservation system is subject to change, so be sure to check the park website before your trip.) There is limited parking at the trailhead but there are other trailhead parking lots along the road. Arrive early for the best luck finding a spot. There are restrooms at both the entrance station and trailhead. The trail can be wet and muddy and there are several creek crossings, so waterproof shoes are ideal for this hike.

Finding the trailhead: From CO 7 in Allenspark, continue north. Turn left on CR 115 for 0.4 mile until you come to the Wild Basin entrance on your right. Continue straight on the narrow dirt road for 2.3 miles until you cross a bridge and come to the end of the road, which is the Wild Basin Trailhead parking lot. GPS: N40 12.47' / W105 33.99'

The Hike

As you hike along North St. Vrain Creek, past Calypso Cascades, and to Ouzel (pronunciation: OO z'l) Falls, keep an eye out for the namesake bird: the water ouzel, or American dipper. This dark gray, robin-sized bird can often be spotted diving into the quickly flowing stream or dipping its head into the water from a rock for aquatic larvae and insects. The famous naturalist and environmentalist John Muir was particularly intrigued by the bird that he first spied in California, writing the following praise in his book *From the Mountains of California* in 1894: "He is the mountain streams' own darling, the humming-bird of blooming waters, loving rocky

Take the path to your left just before the bridge for the best views of the falls.

ripple-slopes and sheets of foam as a bee loves flowers, as a lark loves sunshine and meadows. Among all the mountain birds, none has cheered me so much in my lonely wanderings, —none so unfailingly."

This beautiful hike travels past Engelmann spruce, subalpine fir, lodgepole pine, juniper, aspen, and an abundance of wildflowers. The trail can be wet and muddy, so you'll likely find ferns along the way as well, especially in the earlier section where several rivulets of water cross the trail.

At 0.4 mile, continue straight past the spur trail to Copeland Falls—you'll stop there on your way back. The climb here is a bit rocky. At 1.5 miles, cross a bridge over North St. Vrain Creek for another rocky climb. This time you're immediately rewarded at the top with the beautiful Calypso Cascades. The bridge in front of the falls is a great place to stop for a photo, then continue on to an open hillside, remnants of the 1978 Ouzel Fire. After a lightning strike, winds carried the fire throughout the area, burning more than 1,100 acres in total.

> The water here is stronger and faster than it looks. There are many signs cautioning hikers to stay out of the water, and it's a warning you should heed. Even the rocks can be slippery, so be very careful and stay on the trail.

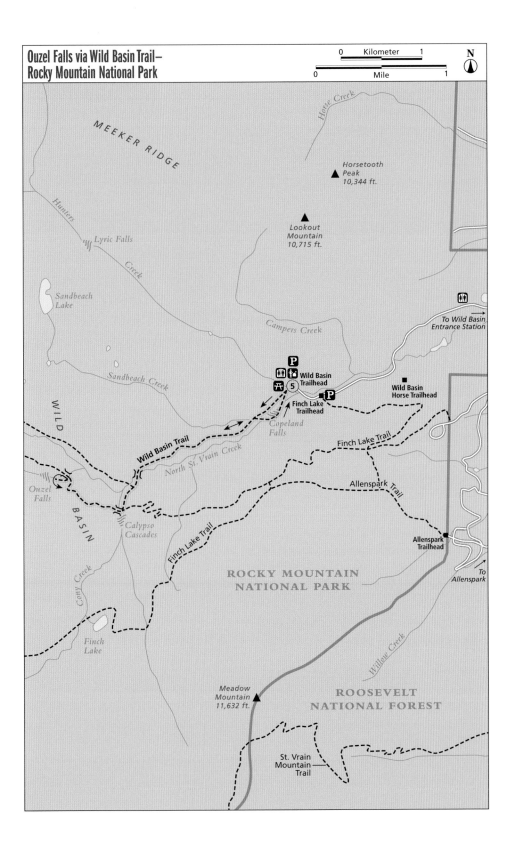

Ouzel Falls via Wild Basin Trail–
Rocky Mountain National Park

0   Kilometer   1

0   Mile   1

N

MEEKER RIDGE

Horse Creek

Horsetooth
Peak
10,344 ft.

Lookout
Mountain
10,715 ft.

Hunters

Lyric Falls

Creek

Sandbeach
Lake

Campers Creek

To Wild Basin
Entrance Station

Sandbeach Creek

Wild Basin
Trailhead

5

Wild Basin
Horse Trailhead

WILD

Finch Lake
Trailhead

Copeland
Falls

Finch Lake Trail

Wild Basin Trail

North St. Vrain Creek

Ouzel
Falls

BASIN

Allenspark Trail

Calypso
Cascades

Finch Lake Trail

Allenspark
Trailhead

Cony Creek

ROCKY MOUNTAIN
NATIONAL PARK

To
Allenspark

Finch
Lake

Willow Creek

Meadow
Mountain
11,632 ft.

ROOSEVELT
NATIONAL FOREST

St. Vrain
Mountain
Trail

Wildflowers are plentiful along this trail, even growing in seemingly inhospitable places!

You'll arrive at Ouzel Falls at around 2.7 miles. There's a large bridge and you may look to your left in excitement, hoping for a perfect shot of the falls. You will not get it from here. The falls tumble south and are mostly hidden by the massive boulders. Just before the bridge on your left there is a spur trail (or at least a clear scramble) that will get you closer and is the spot to get your photo and maybe even stop for a lunch break. On your way back, take the spur trail at 4.9 miles over to Copeland Falls, and then backtrack to the main trail and turn right to finish back at the parking lot.

Miles and Directions

0.0 Start at the Wild Basin Trailhead.

0.4 Go straight at the spur trail to Copeland Falls.

1.5 Cross a bridge over North St. Vrain Creek.

1.8 Arrive at Calypso Cascades. Continue right and across the bridge.

2.7 Arrive at Ouzel Falls. Return the way you came.

4.9 Veer right onto the trail for Copeland Falls.

5.4 Arrive back at the trailhead.

Additional Route Options

If you're looking for a longer trek, continue over the bridge and past Ouzel Falls for an additional 2.3 miles to Ouzel Lake. Here you'll have views of Ouzel Peak and hike a total of 10 miles on the out-and-back. Bluebird Lake is just beyond Ouzel Lake and adds another 1.8 miles through more challenging terrain. Return the way you came back to the trailhead.

6 Finch Lake via Allenspark Trail

The Wild Basin area of the park has a very different vibe than other areas. As the name suggests, it feels more, well, wild. It's rich with wildlife and water features, many named after the wildlife that frequents the area. The area is known as the land of many waters, a name given by Joe Mills (brother of Enos Mills). Finch Lake can be accessed from its namesake trailhead, but the Allenspark Trail cuts down the distance and elevation gain, making it one of the easier lake hikes in Wild Basin.

Start: Allenspark Trailhead
Distance: 7.6 miles out and back
Difficulty: Moderate
Elevation gain: 1,410 feet
Hiking time: 3-4 hours
Trail surface: Dirt for the first mile; rocky the rest of the way to the lake
Seasons/schedule: Summer through fall. The park is open 24/7, weather permitting.
Fees and permits: None. The lake is in Rocky Mountain National Park, but the trail starts outside of park boundaries near the town of Allenspark.

Other trail users: Equestrians
Canine compatibility: No dogs allowed
Land status: Rocky Mountain National Park
Trail contact: Rocky Mountain National Park; (970) 586-1206; www.nps.gov/romo
Maps: USGS Allenspark
Nearest town: Allenspark
Cell service: Spotty
Special considerations: If the parking lot is full, do not block driveways in the residential neighborhood. Bring your hammock to lounge at the lake, or get a permit in advance and set up camp overnight.

Finding the trailhead: From CO 7, turn south on Business 7 (Washington Street) into the town of Allenspark. Drive 1 block and turn right onto CR 90 (portions of this road are unpaved). After 0.7 mile, stay straight to go uphill onto South Skinner Road. After 0.5 mile, turn right onto Meadow Mountain Drive and continue about 0.1 mile to the Allenspark Trailhead parking area on the right. GPS: N40 11.63' / W105 32.54'

The Hike

Shallow Finch Lake sits in a thick forest of lodgepole pine, making for a cool hike with a perfect spot for hanging out in a hammock at the end. Start from the parking lot and follow the sign into the forest for the Allenspark Trail. You'll arrive at the first intersection at 0.8 mile; continue straight.

You're still deep in the trees at this point, and when you come to Confusion Junction at 1.8 miles, stay to the left and follow the sign to Finch Lake. It's here where the

While at the lake, look for the Cassin's finch. The males are a rosy pink and brown with a cream chest and reddish crown, while females are all brown and cream-colored.

The trail opens up for a beautiful view of Finch Lake and Mount Copeland in the distance.

trail gets more difficult—expect a rocky and rooted path the rest of the way. A good distraction is the view of Mount Meeker (13,916 feet) and Longs Peak (14,259 feet).

The grade becomes easier as you follow the path of the 1978 Ouzel Fire, a natural fire started by lightning that proceeded to burn through more than 1,100 acres. The trail meanders through a large stand of charred trees, but you'll also see how the forest has started to rejuvenate itself, with wildflowers, bushes, and new trees growing among the damage. Look for the alpine daisy and the unique elephant's head louse-wort growing here (the purple/pink flowers look like an elephant head, complete with a trunk and big floppy ears!).

When you get to the small bridge over North St. Vrain Creek, you're almost to the lake. From there, the trail drops down to the water and you'll finish at an elevation of 9,910 feet. Return the way you came.

Miles and Directions

0.0 Start at the Allenspark Trailhead parking lot.

0.8 Continue straight to stay on the Allenspark Trail.

1.7 Multiple trails converge here at the aptly named Confusion Junction. Follow the Finch Lake sign and continue on to the Finch Lake Trail by staying all the way to your left.

3.5 Cross a small bridge over North St. Vrain Creek.

3.8 Arrive at Finch Lake. After you've hung out for a while, return the way you came.

7.6 Arrive back at the trailhead.

Finch Lake via Allenspark Trail—Rocky Mountain National Park

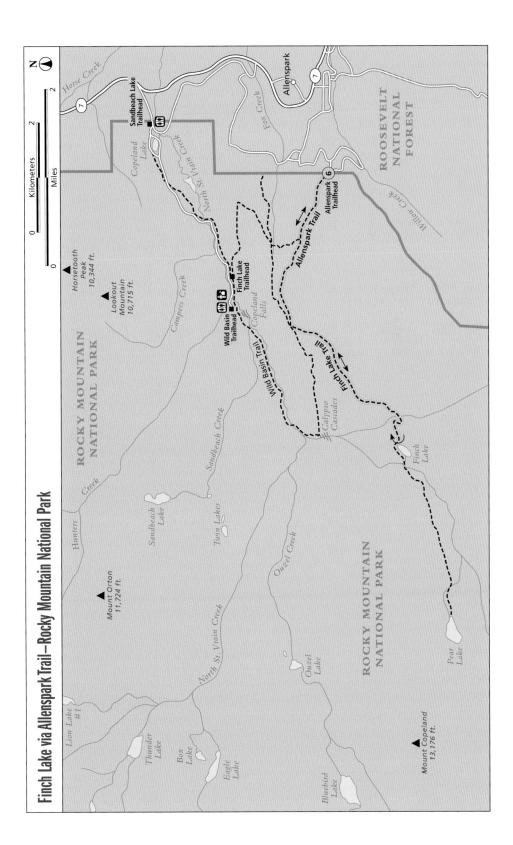

The mix of charred trees from the 1978 Ouzel Fire and new growth offers an interesting landscape with mountain views in the background.

Additional Route Options

Pear Lake is an additional 2 miles (one way) beyond Finch Lake if you'd like to tack on a few additional miles. You'll encounter a steep section or two, but the route is mostly gradual and the elevation gain is only 670 feet as you work your way up to an elevation of 10,580 feet.

Boulder Area

Boulder regularly makes lists as one of the fittest places in the country, and after a drive through town, you'll believe it. I was into all kinds of outdoor activities before moving to Colorado, but I remember the first time I drove along Baseline to go for a hike in Chautauqua Park, I was taken aback by how many people were running, walking, and biking—and CU Boulder was out for the summer at the time!

The area that is now lovingly referred to as the People's Republic of Boulder was inhabited long before the university came to town. For more than 13,000 years, Indigenous people, including the Ute and Arapaho, made their homes here. As recently as the mid-1800s, the Boulder Valley was the winter home and hunting grounds for nomadic bands of Indigenous people. In the fall of 1858, miners in search of gold came to town and called the area Boulder City Town Company. Over the following years, mining grew and the Indigenous people were pushed out. In 1871, Boulder and its 340-plus residents became an incorporated town.

Growth was slow but steady, and in 1877 the University of Colorado, Boulder opened for its first students. By 1900, the town was making a name for itself in the wellness world as a haven for those suffering from tuberculosis. As scientific laboratories and companies came to town (like the National Center for Atmospheric Research and the National Oceanic and Atmospheric Administration) and created more jobs, the population grew and it became apparent that residents needed to take measures to protect the area's natural beauty.

In 1967, voters passed the nation's first municipal sales tax for purchasing and preserving open space. In 1971, a measure passed that banned high-rises and limited buildings to 55 feet. In 1976, a plan narrowly passed to limit growth (which has contributed to the high cost of housing today, but that's another story). The point is, Boulderites have just about always been committed to healthy living and enjoying the outdoors. There are 300 miles of trails in and around Boulder, and in this section I've included a handful of the best. Much like the Rocky Mountain National Park section, there are a few that locals will surely recognize, but some others that have a little less foot traffic.

Boulder's striking, slanted Flatirons are one of the most recognizable features in the state.

7 Davidson Mesa Open Space

It often feels like the space between Denver and Boulder is somewhat forgotten when it comes to getting outdoors. What used to be fields as far as the eye can see is now filled with homes, buildings, and shopping centers. But with that development comes protected spaces, like Davidson Mesa. Located off McCaslin Boulevard between Superior and Louisville, Davidson Mesa Open Space is an easy walk with some of the best views of the Front Range that you'll find anywhere.

Start: Davidson Mesa Trailhead
Distance: 3.4-mile loop
Difficulty: Easy
Elevation gain: 68 feet
Hiking time: 3.5–5 hours
Trail surface: Packed gravel
Seasons/schedule: Year-round; best spring through fall. The trailhead and dog off-leash area is open from 1 hour before sunrise to 1 hour after sunset.
Fees and permits: None
Other trail users: Mountain bikers
Canine compatibility: Dogs allowed on leash on the trail; allowed off-leash in the dog off-leash area
Land status: City of Louisville Open Space

Trail contact: City of Louisville; (303) 666-6565; www.louisvilleco.gov/ Home/Components/FacilityDirectory/ FacilityDirectory/48/15344
Maps: City of Louisville Parks, Recreation & Open Space map
Nearest town: Louisville/Superior
Cell service: Good
Special considerations: The trail is completely exposed, so it can get hot during the summer and is a dangerous place to be if a storm rolls in, so skip this one if there are dark clouds coming or a storm in the forecast. Be sure to bring water. Stay on the trail to protect the native prairie area.

Finding the trailhead: From the intersection of US 36 and Table Mesa Drive, take US 36 east toward Denver for 4.2 miles. Exit onto McCaslin Boulevard. Continue on McCaslin for 1.7 miles until you come to the parking lot on your left. GPS: N39 58.69' / W105 09.99'

The Hike

While much of the land around Davidson Mesa was being developed as farmland, the rocky soil here wasn't suitable for growing, so this patch of native grassland was left alone. The area has been limited to livestock grazing and some gravel extraction. The City of Louisville acquired the 246 acres in 1985 and created the trails for public

Creating social trails (unofficial trails) makes it easier for invasive weeds to grow. Grassland birds are extra sensitive about their nests being disturbed. Stay on the trail to help protect the native prairie here.

The trail has incredible views of the Front Range stretching from north to south.

use. As you walk along the gravel trail, keep an eye out for some of the native flora and fauna: black-tailed prairie dog, western meadowlark, vesper sparrow, yucca moth, and the yucca plant. Coyotes also frequent the mesa in search of mice, rabbits, and prairie dogs.

From the parking lot, follow the trail to the right of the kiosk that heads directly west alongside the off-leash dog area to the north. The closer you get to the back side of the loop, the better the views get. I really enjoy local walks like this that aren't too far away, get you out of town, and give you great views, but these views blew me away. About 0.25 mile into the hike, just past the west boundary of the off-leash space, the trail splits. There is a bench to the south that overlooks the Front Range views. Turn right and then left to stay on the trail and skirt around the perimeter of the open space.

Continue along Davidson Highline Ditch and rejoin the other trail at 0.7 mile. Follow the trail south, parallel with the mountains to your right. Turn right at 1 mile and continue to follow the Davidson Mesa Trail along the neighbor that is next to the open space. Continue on the trail as it curves around to the east. At 1.9 miles, stay left and the trail turns back toward the parking lot. Follow it straight back through

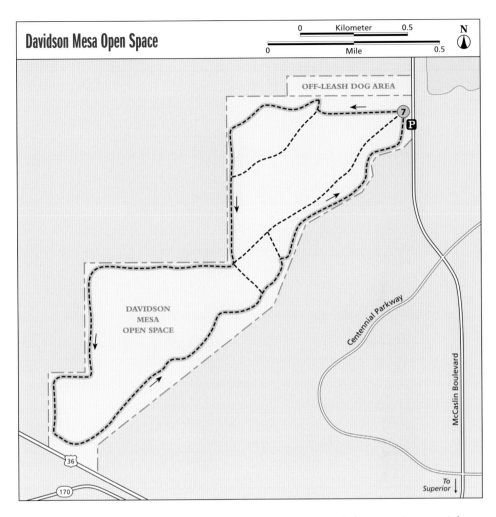

Davidson Mesa Open Space

Kilometer

Mile

N

OFF-LEASH DOG AREA

DAVIDSON
MESA
OPEN SPACE

Centennial Parkway

McCaslin Boulevard

To
Superior

the intersection at 2.6 miles. Turn right at 2.7 miles and then continue straight to your starting point.

Miles and Directions

0.0 Start at the Davidson Mesa Trailhead and walk west to the right of the kiosk.

0.2 Turn right and then left to follow along the Davidson Highline Ditch.

0.6 Continue straight to stay on the Davidson Mesa Trail.

0.8 Turn right to follow the perimeter of the open space.

1.2 Turn left to continue to follow the Davidson Mesa Trail toward US 36.

1.9 Turn left to turn back toward the trailhead.

2.7 Stay straight on the Davidson Mesa Trail.

2.8 Stay straight on the Davidson Mesa Trail.

3.4 Arrive back at the trailhead.

Wildflowers mix in with the prairie grasses.

Additional Route Options

This is the longest option at the open space, but you can cut the walk short by taking any of the trails that shortcut back toward the east.

8 Walker Ranch Loop

The Walker Ranch Loop traverses meadows, rocky ridges, a riparian habitat, and along South Boulder Creek as it winds its way through the open space and Eldorado Canyon State Park. There are plenty of gorgeous views throughout and the landscape is ever-changing, making this a fun and interesting hike. The trail is well marked, with clear signage at intersections and mile markers along the way.

Start: Walker Ranch Loop Trailhead
Distance: 7.9-mile loop
Difficulty: Strenuous
Elevation gain: 1,610 feet
Hiking time: 3.5-5 hours
Trail surface: Mostly dirt, some rocky sections
Seasons/schedule: Year-round; best spring through fall. The park is open from sunrise to sunset.
Fees and permits: None
Other trail users: Mountain bikers and equestrians
Canine compatibility: Dogs allowed on leash

Land status: Boulder County Parks and Open Space; Eldorado Canyon State Park
Trail contact: Boulder County Parks and Open Space; (303) 541-2500; www.bouldercounty .gov/departments/parks-and-open-space
Maps: National Geographic Trails Illustrated #100: Boulder/Golden
Nearest town: Boulder
Cell service: Spotty
Special considerations: The trail is a mix of forest and open sections, so it can get hot during the summer. Be sure to bring extra water. Smoking is prohibited in Boulder County parks.

Finding the trailhead: From the intersection of Broadway (US 93) and Baseline Road in Boulder, drive west on Baseline for 1.4 miles. After Chautauqua Park, Baseline turns into Flagstaff Road. Continue up the steep and winding road for 7.4 miles. Watch for cyclists, especially on the weekends. Turn left into the Walker Ranch Loop parking lot. GPS: N39 57.01' / W105 20.26'

The Hike

From the parking lot, you can see the historical buildings that make up the Walker Ranch Homestead (they're closed to the public except for special events). Now listed as a cultural landscape on the National Register of Historic Places, James Walker and his family once raised livestock, grew potatoes, and logged and milled timber here. What started as 160 acres in 1882 grew to 6,450 acres and remained in the family until 1950. The county purchased 2,566 acres in 1977 and continued adding to it until 2006. The open space stretches to the boundaries of Eldorado Canyon State Park and is home to almost a hundred species of birds, a variety of mammals (mountain lion, black bear, elk, deer, red fox, etc.), bull and garter snakes, and a rich display of colorful wildflowers.

Starting counterclockwise (aka take the trail to your right), head toward the massive boulders straight ahead of you. Before getting to the rocks, you'll bear left and head down into the forest. There are a few wildflowers and plants along the trail here,

Start the Walker Ranch Loop counterclockwise, heading toward the large rocks.

including the mountain mahogany, a perennial shrub. Depending on the season, these may look different: they start with small red blooms that open up and turn yellow, and then finally turn into wispy, silvery strands late in the summer season.

Right around 1 mile, you'll start to hear and see South Boulder Creek to your left. There are some picnic tables down by the water, and it's a nice shady spot for a break. Continue on to the first bridge over the creek and then up a consistent climb until the trail runs parallel to Gross Dam Road. (You'll have also entered Eldorado Canyon State Park during this climb.) From here, turn right and come out of the trees near the Crescent Meadows Trailhead and parking lot (this one is closer to those coming from Denver versus Boulder).

South Boulder Creek starts high in the mountains beneath the Continental Divide and is fed by snowmelt. The water you see in front of you flows 40 miles from the peaks to the plains and continues on to the Gulf of Mexico. The creek supports a diverse ecosystem of aquatic insects that feed trout and the gray water ouzel, or American dipper. Mule deer and red foxes drink from the banks, and it supplies water to humans in Boulder County and beyond.

Two different sections of the loop run along and across South Boulder Creek.

After dropping back into the forest via a series of wooden steps, you'll come around a corner and reunite with South Boulder Creek. There are plenty of spots here to pause and enjoy the sounds of the water, from large boulders to a bench. You then cross the East Bridge. The next mile has an intersection with a trail in Eldorado Canyon State Park and Ethel Harrold Road; follow the signs to stay on the Walker Ranch Loop. As you come back up, be sure to stop just after the 7-mile marker when the trail opens up and turn around for views through Eldorado Canyon to the plains. The last mile is fairly exposed, but there are plenty of flowers lining the trail and cheering you on to the finish.

Miles and Directions

0.0   Start at the Walker Ranch Loop Trailhead and take the path to the right.

0.2   Follow the trail to the left.

0.5   A spur trail leads to a bench with a view.

1.0   A spur trail leads down to a picnic area by the water.

1.4   Cross the West Bridge over South Boulder Creek.

1.7   Follow the trail to the right.

2.4   Follow the trail up and to the left.

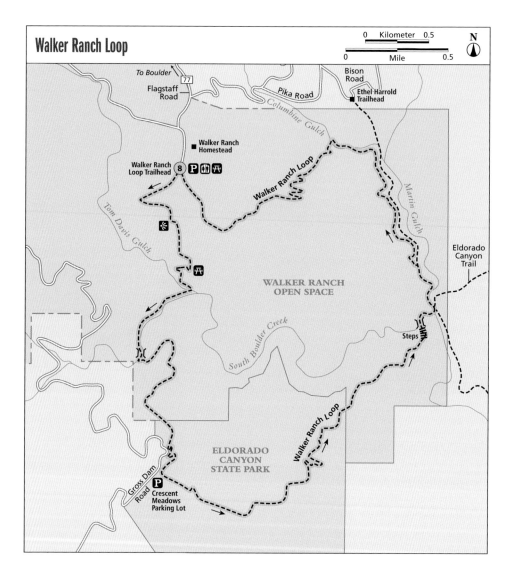

Walker Ranch Loop

0 Kilometer 0.5

0 Mile 0.5

N

To Boulder
Flagstaff Road
77
Bison Road
Pika Road
Ethel Harrold Trailhead
Columbine Gulch

Walker Ranch Homestead

Walker Ranch Loop Trailhead 8 P 🚻 🏕

Walker Ranch Loop

Tom Davis Gulch

Martin Gulch

Eldorado Canyon Trail

WALKER RANCH OPEN SPACE

South Boulder Creek

Steps

Walker Ranch Loop

ELDORADO CANYON STATE PARK

Gross Dam Road
P
Crescent Meadows Parking Lot

2.5 Pass the Crescent Meadows parking lot (there are no services here).

4.4 The trail splits and there is a sign indicating that the higher route to your left is less technical. It also has better views!

4.7 There are many steps here. They are well made with dirt, rock, and wood but take your time. At the bottom, follow the creek to the right and cross the East Bridge.

4.9 Arrive at a metal fence on your right, which marks the boundary of the open space. Turn left to follow the wider road.

5.0 Stay straight on the Walker Ranch Loop.

5.2 Come to an intersection with Ethel Harrold Road; follow the signs and turn left.

6.1 Cross a rock bridge and come to the intersection with the Ethel Harrold Trail. Go left.

Wide-open views just after mile 7—there's even a bench to sit on!

7.1 Come to a bench with views of the plains and the trail you've—almost—completed.

7.9 Arrive back at the trailhead.

Additional Route Options

For a longer day trip, add on the Eldorado Canyon Trail. The intersection is at mile 5 and can add up to 7 miles (out and back).

$\bigcirc$ Royal Arch Trail

This trail is not for the faint of heart—or those not acclimated to elevation—but the views are worth the effort. The hike is (mercifully) not very long but is a popular trail in Boulder because it packs quite a punch. Several trails crisscross through the area, so it's important to pay attention to the directions and signage unless you want to add on more mileage.

Start: Chautauqua Park Trailhead
Distance: 3.5 miles out and back
Difficulty: Strenuous
Elevation gain: 1,437 feet
Hiking time: 2–3 hours
Trail surface: Rocky
Seasons/schedule: Summer through fall. The park is open daily from 5 a.m. to 11 p.m.
Fees and permits: Parking is free in the fall, winter, and spring. From Memorial Day through Labor Day, there is a fee from 8 a.m. to 5 p.m. on weekends and holidays along the Chautauqua Park green parking areas, on Baseline Road near the park, at the Chautauqua Ranger Cottage lot, and in the neighborhood north of Chautauqua Park. There is a free park shuttle on summer weekends. Learn more at www.bouldercolorado.gov/services/park-to-park-shuttle.
Other trail users: None
Canine compatibility: Dogs allowed on leash
Land status: Boulder Open Space and Mountain Parks
Trail contact: Boulder County Parks and Open Space; (303) 541-2500; www.bouldercounty.gov/departments/parks-and-open-space
Maps: OSMP Trail Map
Nearest town: Boulder
Cell service: Good
Special considerations: This is a popular trail, especially on summer weekends, so plan ahead to get there early or take the shuttle. Smoking is prohibited in Boulder County parks.

Finding the trailhead: From the intersection of Broadway (US 93) and Baseline Road in Boulder, drive west on Baseline for 1 mile. Turn left on Kinnikinnick Road into the Chautauqua Park parking lot. GPS: N39 59.93' / W105 16.99'

The Hike

The Colorado Chautauqua was part of the Chautauqua movement that originated in the late nineteenth century in Chautauqua, New York. The movement swept across the country and found a home in Boulder in 1898 when residents were interested in creating an educational and cultural center. It became a popular spot for summer programs and community gatherings, and was the only Chautauqua west of the Mississippi. Today, the park is a National Historic Landmark and continues to host events and offer lodging, and also has a dining hall, general store, public restrooms, and access to 40 miles of trails.

From the parking lot, start walking south (left) on Bluebell Road, a wide dirt path for foot traffic only. The gradual incline leads to a restroom building just after 0.5 mile

The arch is a unique natural feature in the Front Range. JACOB PREBLE

Patches of sweet pea flowers can be found along Bluebell Road en route to the Royal Arch.

and the Bluebell Shelter. Take the path that leads left after the Bluebell Shelter sign and head into the mixed pine forest. You'll come to a sign that lists the trails in the area; go straight to the Royal Arch Trail.

After crossing a bridge, you'll start a pattern of going up and leveling out until about a mile, when it's a continuous climb for the rest of the trail to get out of the narrow gulch and to Sentinel Pass at the top of Bluebell Canyon. There are rooty inclines, rocky steps, a little scrambling, and then finally pushing up to the arch just after 1.7 miles. A couple spots along the way offer views through the trees of Boulder, and don't be fooled by the false summit at 1.4 miles in. On a clear day you can see as far as Denver, some 25-plus miles south. As you turn around and come back, you'll see part of the 3rd Flatiron through the arch.

The Flatirons are one of the most famous natural landmarks in the state, part of the Fountain Formation. The Fountain Formation was created about 280 million years ago, as part of the eroded materials from the Ancestral Rocky Mountains. The Flatirons were initially flat against the ground, but were tilted during a major uplift process approximately 65 million years ago.

You can scramble over the rocks and through the arch to take a break and take in the views of Boulder, depending on how many fellow hikers are up there. When

The Royal Arch Trail offers views of Boulder, the Flatirons, and beyond.

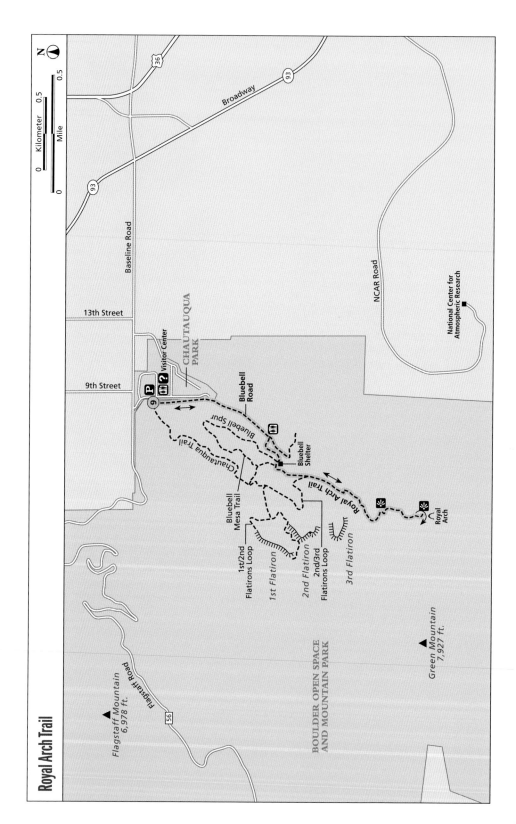

Royal Arch Trail

Flagstaff Mountain
6,978 ft.

Flagstaff Road

56

BOULDER OPEN SPACE
AND MOUNTAIN PARK

Green Mountain
7,927 ft.

1st/2nd
Flatirons Loop

1st Flatiron

2nd Flatiron

2nd/3rd
Flatirons Loop

3rd Flatiron

Bluebell
Mesa Trail

Chautauqua Trail

Bluebell Spur

Royal Arch Trail

Royal
Arch

Bluebell Shelter

Bluebell Road

Visitor Center

CHAUTAUQUA PARK

9th Street

13th Street

Baseline Road

P

9

93

93

36

Broadway

NCAR Road

National Center for
Atmospheric Research

N

Kilometer   0   0.5
Mile   0   0.5

you're ready to head back down, follow the same route back. At miles 2.5 and 2.7, make sure you stay to the right.

Miles and Directions

0.0 Start at the Chautauqua Park Trailhead and go left up Bluebell Road.

0.5 Stay right as you go past the restrooms, then bear left past the Bluebell Shelter.

0.7 Follow signs for the Royal Arch Trail and cross a bridge.

0.9 Stay straight.

1.1 Follow the obvious trail through the talus.

1.7 Arrive at the Royal Arch. Retrace your steps to return to the trailhead.

2.5 Stay right.

2.7 Stay right and downhill then to the right when you get back to the Royal Arch Trail.

3.5 Arrive back at the trailhead.

Additional Route Options

There is a high concentration of trails in this area of Chautauqua Park. A 2.5-mile trail combination that isn't as strenuous but includes the Royal Arch is the Bluebell, Royal Arch, Flatiron, Bluebell–Baird, and Meadow Trail Loop. If you're up for the challenge and want to add on more mileage, take a left either on your way up (0.9 mile) or on your way back (2.5 miles) and hit the Flatirons Loop to add about 2.5 to 3 miles to your hike.

10 Sugarloaf Mountain

Don't let the low mileage fool you—this is a difficult, rocky climb just over 0.5 mile up to the top of Sugarloaf Mountain at 8,912 feet. At the top, you'll have expansive views of the Indian Peaks Wilderness, Rocky Mountain National Park, James Peak Wilderness, the town of Boulder, and all the way to the plains.

Start: Switzerland Trail parking lot
Distance: 1.4 miles out and back
Difficulty: Strenuous
Elevation gain: 439 feet
Hiking time: 1 hour or less
Trail surface: Rocky
Seasons/schedule: Year-round
Fees and permits: None
Other trail users: Mountain bikers
Canine compatibility: Dogs allowed on leash

Land status: Roosevelt National Forest
Trail contact: Boulder Ranger District; (303) 541-2500; www.fs.usda.gov/recarea/arp/recarea/?recid=28178
Maps: National Geographic Trails Illustrated #104: Indian Peaks/Gold Hill
Nearest town: Boulder
Cell Service: None at trailhead or in Boulder Canyon
Special considerations: None

Finding the trailhead: From the intersection of Broadway (US 93) and Boulder Canyon Drive (CO 119) in Boulder, drive west on Boulder Canyon Drive through the windy canyon for 5.2 miles. Turn right onto Sugarloaf Road and follow it up for 4.7 miles. Turn right onto the dirt Sugarloaf Mountain Road to the parking lot in 0.8 mile. The trailhead will be on your right. GPS: N40 01.50' / W105 25.49'

The Hike

The main trailhead at this parking lot is the Switzerland Trail of America, an abandoned railroad line overlapping with FR 93. The line originally brought supplies to the mining camps in the area but turned into a route for tourists too. In 1881, the Greeley, Salt Lake & Pacific Railroad ran from Boulder to the town of Sunset. The town and the railroad are long gone due to the collapse of the mining industry after World War I, but Sugarloaf is still a thriving mountain community from those days. Dating back to 1860, it's not clear where exactly the name came from, but it was likely either a mining claim or a term for a mining district. Even today, you can see the shiny glint of the minerals in the rocks as you climb the trail to the top of the mountain.

The view from the Sugarloaf Mountain Trail of the peaks in the distance.

From the parking lot, you'll see the wide Switzerland Trail to the north and west. The hike up Sugarloaf Mountain starts on the east side of the parking lot. There are two ways to access the trail: one is by the green post that has the number 800 on it, and the other is past the No Motor Vehicles sign and the gate beyond.

Either way, start climbing the rocky trail. A couple other social trails will join in at 0.1 and 0.3 mile, but continue following the wider, rockier trail. You'll pass through some lovely aspens and just enough trees to partially block the views. Once you get to the top, take a break to enjoy 360-degree vistas before heading back down the way you came.

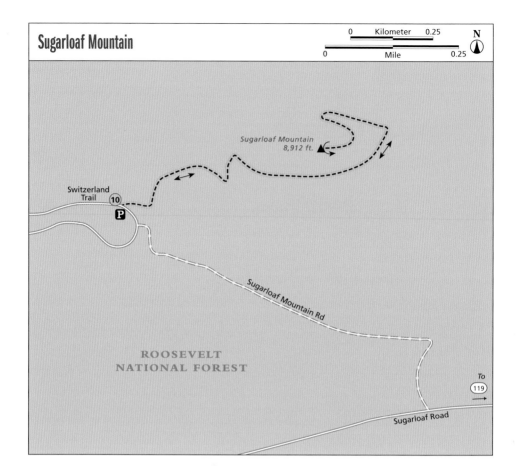

Switzerland
Trail ⑩
🅿

Sugarloaf Mountain
8,912 ft.

Sugarloaf Mountain Rd

ROOSEVELT
NATIONAL FOREST

To
⑪⑨

Sugarloaf Road

0   Kilometer   0.25   N
0   Mile   0.25

Miles and Directions

0.0   Start at the trailhead on the east side of the parking lot and go east up the Sugarloaf
Mountain Trail.

0.1   Stay to the left.

0.3   Stay to the left.

0.7   Arrive at the peak.

1.4   Arrive back at the trailhead.

11 Wapiti and Ponderosa Loop Trails

Heil Valley Ranch, where this hike is located, is rich in wildlife and geologic history. More than fifty species of mammals and almost a hundred species of birds live here, while the ranch showcases the landscape where the plains and the Front Range meet. This loop takes you along burn areas from 2003 and 2020, through meadows, and past ponderosa pines to picturesque views of Mount Meeker (13,811 feet) and Longs Peak (14,251 feet).

Start: Main Trailhead
Distance: 7.6-mile lollipop
Difficulty: Moderate
Elevation gain: 1,046 feet
Hiking time: 2.5–3.5 hours
Trail surface: Dirt and rocks
Seasons/schedule: Year-round. The park is day use only and open from sunrise to sunset.
Fees and permits: None
Other trail users: Mountain bikers
Canine compatibility: No dogs allowed
Land status: Boulder Open Space and Mountain Parks

Trail contact: Boulder County Parks and Open Space; (303) 678-6200; www.boulder county.gov/open-space/parks-and-trails/ heil-valley-ranch
Maps: Heil Valley Ranch map
Nearest town: Boulder
Cell service: None
Special considerations: The Main Trailhead parking lot may be closed if there is the potential for heavy rains, flashing flooding, or debris flow.

Finding the trailhead: From the intersection of 28th Street (US 36) and Canyon Boulevard (CO 119) in Boulder, drive north on US 36 for 8.6 miles. Turn left onto Lefthand Canyon Drive for 0.7 mile, then turn right onto Geer Canyon Drive for 1.2 miles. Turn right into Heil Valley Ranch and continue for 0.2 mile until you reach the Main Trailhead parking lot. GPS: N40 08.97' / W105 18.03'

The Hike

The human history of Heil Valley Ranch dates back 5,000 years, followed by beaver trappers in the late eighteenth and nineteenth centuries. The historical sites at the ranch go back to the quarry operations from the 1890s to the 1960s. But like the rest of the Front Range, the geologic history of Heil Valley Ranch goes back millions of years. On the east side of the property is a hogback, part of the Dakota Formation. On the west side is Lyons Sandstone, which is the same formation that makes up the Garden of the Gods' red sandstone formations.

Today, many animals can be found here, from the all-black Abert's squirrel to the western scrub jay and wild turkeys. It's an important winter home for migrating elk as they make their way from the Indian Peaks Wilderness out to the plains. Plenty of plants grow here as well, including the purple bells of the penstemon, juniper, bee balm, mariposa lily, and silvery lupine.

The trail starts at a burn area from the 2003 and 2020 fires.

But the first thing you'll notice when you start this trail is the black burned trees along a good portion of the route. Fueled by strong winds, the Overland Fire in 2003 and the Cal-Wood Fire raged through the area in 2020. Recovery work continues from the 2020 burn, and a section of the Wapiti Trail remains rerouted. This is because a pair of golden eagles rebuilt their burned nest and had a fledgling during the 2020–2021 season. The pair returned for 2021–2022 and are expected to return each year, and Colorado Parks & Wildlife and the US Fish and Wildlife Service are evaluating whether or not to make the detour permanent.

From the parking lot, set out on the Wapiti Trail, which is at the north end of the lot, left of the Lichen Loop. Just after 0.5 mile, the Lichen Loop will come in from the right. Shortly after this is the detour from the old path; continue straight here. At 2.5 miles, you'll connect with the Ponderosa Loop. Go straight to start the loop counterclockwise and then continue straight at 2.7 miles. After another mile, you'll come to a scenic overlook. Finish the loop at 5.1 miles and return the way you came on the Wapiti Trail.

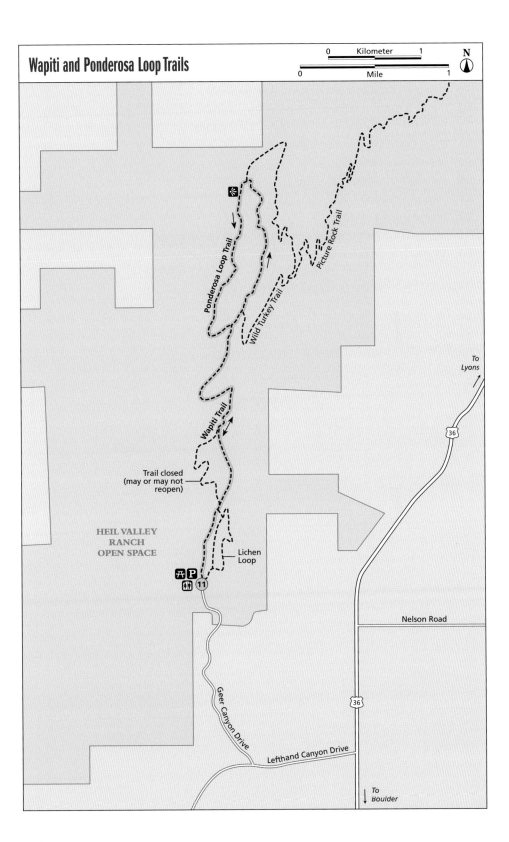

Wapiti and Ponderosa Loop Trails

Kilometer
0   1

Mile
0   1

N

Ponderosa Loop Trail

Wild Turkey Trail

Picture Rock Trail

To
Lyons

36

Wapiti Trail

Trail closed
(may or may not
reopen)

HEIL VALLEY
RANCH
OPEN SPACE

Lichen
Loop

11

Nelson Road

Geer Canyon Drive

36

Lefthand Canyon Drive

To
Boulder

Miles and Directions

0.0   Start at the trailhead on the north end of the parking lot.

0.3   Cross a bridge

0.5   The Lichen Loop comes in from the right; continue straight.

0.6   Follow the detour to stay on the Wapiti Trail.

1.2   Cross an old service road.

2.5   Go straight on the Ponderosa Loop.

3.3   Cross an old service road.

3.7   Arrive at a scenic overlook.

5.1   Reconnect with the Wapiti Trail; turn right and return the way you came.

7.6   Arrive back at the trailhead.

Additional Route Options

There are other trails that you can connect to for more mileage. The Wild Turkey Trail adds another 2.9 miles. You can connect with it at the top of the Ponderosa Loop before the viewpoint. Another option is to take the Picture Rock Trail out to the north end of the park. It's 5.2 miles one way and features the Whitestone and Vickery Quarry Complex.

ENCOUNTERS WITH NATURE: MOUNTAIN LIONS

Mountain lions, also called cougars, generally keep to themselves, living in remote areas with plenty of places to hide. Unfortunately, the number of human interactions with mountain lions has increased over the years, due to things like development of the lions' habitat, increase in deer populations (their primary source of food), more people recreating in mountain lion habitats, and an increase in the mountain lion population.

Adult mountain lions can weigh between 90 and 175 pounds and range from 7 to 8 feet long. Attacks are rare, and are usually by young lions who are going for easy prey like pets or small children. Do not hike alone in mountain lion country and consider bringing a hiking stick or something that could be used if you need to defend yourself. If you do come across a mountain lion:

- Never approach the animal, especially one that has babies. Mountain lions usually try to avoid confrontation, so let it escape.
- Stay calm and speak firmly. Do not yell or scream at the lion.
- Back away slowly, standing upright. Do not run or it may instinctually chase you.
- Try to appear larger: raise your arms, open your jacket. If you have small children with you, pick them up.
- If the lion starts to aggressively come at you, throw stones, branches, or whatever you can without crouching down or turning your back on it.
- If the lion attacks you, fight back. Remain standing or try to get back up if you get knocked down. Mountain lions may leave if the "prey" fights back.

If you have an encounter or are attacked, call Colorado Parks & Wildlife immediately at (303) 297-1192 (main headquarters in Denver) or (719) 227-5200 (regional office in Colorado Springs). If the incident occurs after 5 p.m. or on a weekend, call the Colorado State Patrol at (303) 239-4501.

A sign warning of mountain lions at Heil Valley Ranch.

12 Caribou Ranch Loop

The Caribou Ranch Loop isn't as popular as some of the other trails in and around Nederland, but it has a lot to offer. The route goes through open meadows and ponderosa pine and Douglas fir forest, along the Switzerland Trail of America, past an old homestead from the 1860s, to an old mine complex, and finishes at a small waterfall. The stands of aspens throughout this hike are especially beautiful in the fall.

Start: Caribou Ranch Open Space parking lot
Distance: 4.9-mile lollipop
Difficulty: Easy
Elevation gain: 1,437 feet
Hiking time: 2-3 hours
Trail surface: Dirt
Seasons/schedule: Summer through fall; the open space is closed from April 1 through June 30 to protect migratory birds and elk. When open, hours are sunrise to sunset.
Fees and permits: None
Other trail users: Equestrians
Canine compatibility: Dogs not allowed
Land status: Boulder County Parks and Open Space
Trail contact: Boulder County Parks and Open Space; (303) 678-6200; www.bouldercounty .gov/departments/parks-and-open-space

Maps: National Geographic Trails Illustrated #102: Indian Peaks/Gold Hill
Nearest town: Nederland
Cell service: Spotty on trail; none on road to parking lot
Special considerations: If the parking lot is full, you may park on the south side of CR 126, west of the trailhead. The trail is marked with a blue diamond symbol. Caribou Ranch Open Space is in the heart of moose country—read the signage at the trailhead for tips on moose safety. There can be blackflies in the meadow area close to the trailhead; you may want to bring bug spray or an essential oil–based repellent like Para'kito that you can just clip on your pack to keep the bugs away.

Finding the trailhead: From the intersection of 28th Street (US 36) and Canyon Boulevard (CO 119) in Boulder, head west on CO 119 for 18 miles. When you get to Nederland, take the second exit at the roundabout to turn right onto CO 72 toward Estes Park. Drive 1.7 miles and turn left on CR 126. Follow CR 126 for 0.9 mile to the parking lot of Caribou Ranch Open Space, which will be on your right. GPS: N39 58.95' / W105 31.22'

The Hike

Starting from the parking lot, walk the easy path through the aspen- and wildflower-filled meadow to the junction with the old Switzerland Trail rail bed. Turn right and look for an interpretive sign on the left. Back in 1898, the Colorado & Northwestern Railway (C&N) transported visitors, miners, and materials the 26.1 miles between Boulder and Ward. The line was named the Switzerland Trail after more and more visitors commented on the unparalleled alpine views along the route. Over time, mining towns turned into ghost towns and automobiles became the main mode of

The valley where the DeLonde Homestead sits looks very much the same as it did in 1870.

transportation. On October 1, 1920, Boulder's *Daily Camera* newspaper reported, "The Switzerland Trail is no more." As you walk the old rail bed, imagine Locomotive #30 rolling into milepost 26.7 at the Blue Bird Mine.

At 1.2 miles, you'll come to the beginning of the loop. Turn right toward the Artist Residence and DeLonde Homestead. The DeLande (original spelling) brothers arrived in the area in 1863 to join the miners in search of silver ore. They eventually changed their focus to ranching and haying in the meadows around the property. In 1936, Lynn and Rose Van Vleet purchased part of the property and opened the Lazy VV Ranch, the first Arabian horse ranch in the state. After the Van Vleets sold the ranch, many ideas were thrown around for the property, but it wasn't used for anything until a music producer built a recording studio in 1971. Names such as John Lennon, Joe Walsh, Chicago, Elton John, Michael Jackson, and Rod Stewart produced albums there. Unfortunately, the studio burned down in a fire in 1985 and was never rebuilt.

Continue past the Artist-in-Residence home and into the forest. At 2 miles, the trail continues to the left but there is a spur trail with a few steps down to the water. Shortly after, the trail splits; take a right to go up to the Blue Bird Mine complex. Open from the 1870s until the 1960s, miners flocked to the area in search of silver ore. There are several buildings here, plus the entrance to the original mine tunnel.

The Blue Bird Mine complex was open from the 1870s to 1960s.

Many of the buildings are closed or blocked off for your safety, so do not climb or try to enter any of these areas. In the early 1900s, the complex was a whistle stop for the Denver, Boulder & Western Railroad. The mine also attracted attention from Hollywood: it was the site of two Warner Brothers films in the 1940s (*Arabians of the Rockies* and *Sons of Courage*). The bunkhouse here was also a stagecoach stop in the 1965 remake of *Stagecoach*, featuring Bing Crosby and Ann Margaret.

Walk through the mine complex to a small waterfall at the boundary of the open space. Retrace your steps through the mine complex and follow the trail to the right to finish the loop and head back through the aspens to your starting point.

The red house that stands out among the green meadow grass is part of the Artist-in-Residence Program at Caribou Ranch. According to the sign, it "provides an opportunity for artists to pursue their work in the inspiring landscape and history of Caribou Ranch." The program is open to artists of all kinds, including musicians, painters, photographers, sculptors, writers, and poets. In return, the artists are required to donate a piece of their work to Boulder County for future generations to enjoy.

Caribou Ranch Loop

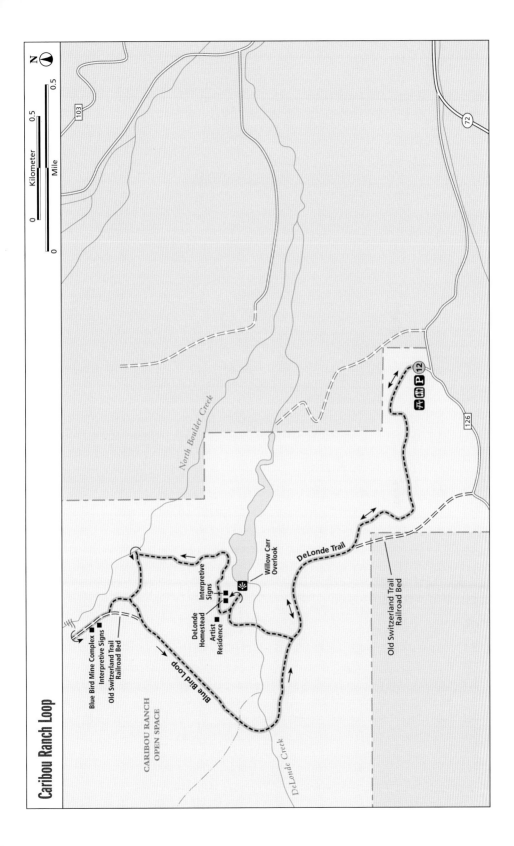

Blue Bird Mine Complex
Interpretive Signs
Old Switzerland Trail Railroad Bed

CARIBOU RANCH OPEN SPACE

Blue Bird Loop

DeLonde Creek

DeLonde Homestead
Artist Residence
Interpretive Signs

Willow Carr Overlook

DeLonde Trail

Old Switzerland Trail Railroad Bed

North Boulder Creek

103

72

126

12

N

Kilometer
0   0.5

Mile
0   0.5

The stands of aspens throughout make this a beautiful hike (or run!), especially when the leaves change to bright yellow and orange hues in the fall.

Miles and Directions

0.0   Start at the trailhead at the Caribou Ranch Open Space parking lot.

0.8   Come to the junction with the old Switzerland Trail railroad bed and turn right.

1.2   Turn right onto the Blue Bird Loop.

1.4   At the DeLonde Homestead, take the 0.2-mile spur trail to the right to the Willow Carr Overlook. If you go to the overlook, return the way you came to rejoin the DeLonde Trail. Bear to the right and go past the red house.

1.8   Arrive at a gate that designates private property. Continue on the trail as it curves to the left.

2.0   A small spur trail to the right leads down to the water.

2.2   The trail splits; turn right and walk 0.1 mile to the Blue Bird Mine complex.

2.6   Arrive at the small waterfall. Retrace your steps back through the mine complex.

2.9   Go right on the dirt path that splits away from the complex instead of the dirt path to the left where you initially came from.

3.7   Rejoin the DeLonde Trail and continue straight.

4.1   Turn left to stay on the DeLonde Trail and return to the trailhead.

4.9   Arrive back at the trailhead.

13 Lake Isabelle via Pawnee Pass Trail

The hike to Lake Isabelle is one of my absolute favorites. You'll travel through meadow and forest, along lakes and streams, and the pièce de résistance is a high-alpine lake nestled beneath Isabelle Glacier. This trail is at a higher elevation, topping out at 10,893 feet, but with minimal elevation gain, the hike is accessible to most if you just take your time.

Start: Niwot Cutoff Trailhead
Distance: 6.6 miles out and back
Difficulty: Moderate
Elevation gain: 672 feet
Hiking time: 2–3 hours
Trail surface: Mostly dirt, some rocky sections closer to the lake
Seasons/schedule: Late summer through fall
Fees and permits: Daily entrance fee or America the Beautiful annual pass is required. You'll also need a timed reservation from early June through mid-October (the summer operating season), available at recreation.gov. There is no fee to park at the Gateway Trailhead and enter Brainard Lake Recreation Area by foot or bike.
Other trail users: None
Canine compatibility: Dogs allowed on leash
Land status: Roosevelt National Forest; Indian Peaks Wilderness
Trail contact: Boulder Ranger District; (303) 541-2500; www.fs.usda.gov/recarea/arp/recarea/?recid=28178

Maps: National Geographic Trails Illustrated #102: Indian Peaks/Gold Hill
Nearest town: Ward
Cell service: None
Special considerations: This is a popular trail, especially on summer weekends, and reservations are released two weeks in advance. Camping is prohibited on this trail between May 1 and November 30. Due to the elevation, snow can remain on the trail until July and the trailhead may not open until July 1. Once the gate opens for the summer season, the recreation area is open 24 hours a day. The Long Lake Trailhead is closer to the Niwot Cutoff Trailhead than the main parking lot, but this lot only has parking for 14 cars and fills up quickly. The Niwot Picnic Site is directly across from the trailhead but only has space for 8 cars. Moose are common in Brainard Lake Recreation Area. Read the signage at the trailhead for safety tips.

Finding the trailhead: From the intersection of 28th Street (US 36) and Canyon Boulevard (CO 119) in Boulder, head west on CO 119 for 18 miles. When you get to Nederland, take the second exit at the roundabout to turn right onto CO 72 toward Estes Park. Drive 11.5 miles, then turn left onto Brainard Lake Road. It's 2.6 miles to the entrance station and then about 2 more miles to the main parking area. GPS: N40 04.49' / W105 34.65'

The Hike

Wherever you park, make your way to the Niwot Picnic Site. Cross Brainard Lake Road and find the obvious trailhead. The trail starts with a rather robust uphill through the trees, but don't let it fool you into thinking that this is a strenuous hike—it will

Lake Isabelle is a gorgeous alpine lake below Isabelle Glacier.

level out after just 0.25 mile and open up to a lovely meadow with mountain views in the distance.

At 0.6 mile, you'll enter the Indian Peaks Wilderness and reach an intersection with the loop around Long Lake. I suggest going straight onto the Jean Lunning Trail first, as it has several viewpoints between the trees. The trail can be muddy and you'll cross several boardwalks over streams running down to the lake. At 1.6 miles, there's a larger bridge over South St. Vrain Creek and you can get a look between the trees of the peaks that loom over your final destination.

Just before 2 miles, you'll reach a junction with the Pawnee Pass Trail. Turn left for a short uphill and another bridge. The trail opens up to a meadow surrounded by subalpine forest. It starts to get a little rocky here, with some stone steps and a log

Before the 2000s, you'd be hard-pressed to find moose in Colorado. Twenty-four male and female moose from Wyoming and Utah were introduced into the state in 1978, and the population has since grown to nearly 3,000. Today, the state's moose population is thriving so much that there are even a limited number of seasonal hunting permits issued now.

Moose, deer, and elk are all frequently spotted in the Indian Peaks Wilderness near Brainard Lake.

creek crossing (the waterfall uphill to your right is beautiful!). Continue straight on the Isabelle Glacier Trail and the lake will appear in front of you. Stay high and to the right to continue around the lake, or take any of the spur trails down to the water.

All the way on the west side of the lake is Isabelle Glacier, source of South St. Vrain Creek. The glacier sits in a cirque basin framed by Shoshone, Apache, and Navajo Peaks. Come back the way you came, except stay on the Pawnee Pass Trail at Long Lake. Once you pass the lake at mile 5, take a right and cross the bridge. You'll soon arrive back at the Indian Peaks Wilderness sign. Turn left to get back on the Niwot Cutoff Trail and return to the trailhead.

Miles and Directions

0.0 Start at the Niwot Cutoff Trailhead.

0.6 Cross into the Indian Peaks Wilderness; continue straight onto the Jean Lunning Trail.

Lake Isabelle via Pawnee Pass Trail

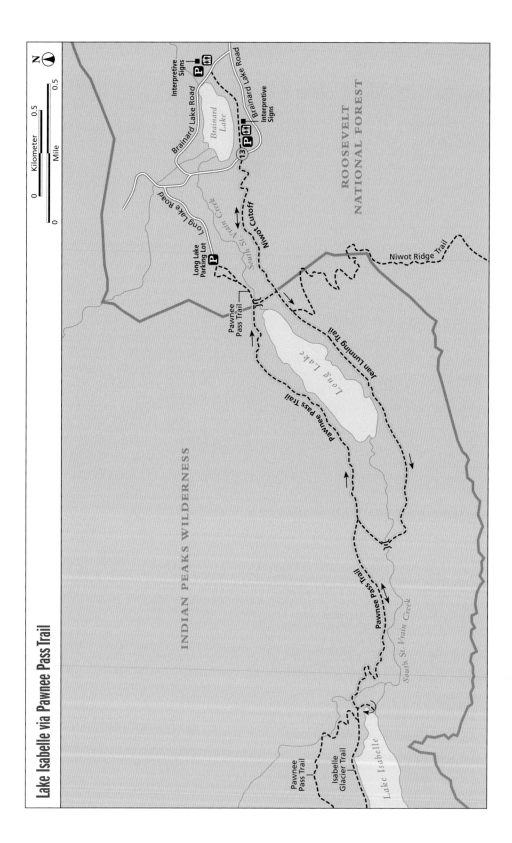

There is no shortage of mountain views on this hike.

0.7 Stay straight on the Jean Lunning Trail.

1.9 Turn left onto the Pawnee Pass Trail.

2.9 Go straight onto the Isabelle Glacier Trail. Arrive at Isabelle Lake and return the way you came.

4.0 Go straight to stay on the Pawnee Pass Trail.

5.0 Turn right and go over the bridge. (*Note:* If you parked in the Long Lake parking lot, you could go straight here for a shortcut back to your parking spot.)

5.1 Come to the intersection with the Jean Lunning Trail; turn left.

6.6 Arrive back at the trailhead.

Additional Route Options

For an added challenge, continue past Lake Isabelle to Isabelle Glacier. You'll add 2 more miles to the round-trip distance and 1,107 more feet of elevation gain for a high point of 12,000 feet. If you decide to push all the way to the glacier, start your hike early enough to get up and back before any afternoon storm might roll in.

ENCOUNTERS WITH NATURE: MOOSE

Twenty years ago, it was hard to find a moose in Colorado. Now that the state's population has rebounded, it's more likely that you'll run into one while hiking, especially at places like Brainard Lake Recreation Area or Caribou Ranch Open Space.

Moose are huge, standing up to 6 feet at the shoulder and weighing 800 to 1,200 pounds. Unlike elk or deer, moose rumps are brown, not white or cream-colored. Their hair may appear black from a distance, and their legs seem almost comically long and skinny compared to their body. Bull moose antlers can reach up to 5 feet wide or larger, while younger bulls have small spikes that eventually grow into the characteristic antlers. Breeding season runs from mid- to late September until October, and during this time bulls can be very territorial.

Moose aren't inherently aggressive but will charge if they perceive you to be a threat, especially during breeding season or if a calf is around. If you do end up too close to a moose, take the following steps:

- If the moose hasn't noticed you yet, quietly move away.
- If the moose has noticed you, speak softly and move away slowly.
- Don't yell or throw anything at the moose—you want to convince it that you aren't a threat.
- If you think the moose is going to charge, take cover behind something like a car or tree or run away.

You can tell the moose is upset if its ears are back and hackles are up. Unlike with bears or mountain lions, it's okay to run away from a moose. They won't likely chase you and if they do, it will probably just be for a short while as a warning.

A sign warning of moose at Caribou Ranch Open Space.

14 Ceran St. Vrain Trail to Miller Rock

This lovely trail meanders through a lodgepole pine forest along South St. Vrain Creek with plenty of places to stop by the water. The climb to Miller Rock is a tough one, but you'll get wide-open views that stretch all the way to Rocky Mountain National Park.

Start: Ceran St. Vrain Trailhead
Distance: 6-mile lollipop
Difficulty: Easy along the Ceran St. Vrain Trail and then a strenuous climb up to Miller Rock
Elevation gain: 981 feet
Hiking time: 2.5-3.5 hours
Trail surface: Dirt and rock
Seasons/schedule: Late spring through fall
Fees and permits: None
Other trail users: Mountain bikers and equestrians
Canine compatibility: Dogs allowed on leash
Land status: Arapaho and Roosevelt National Forests
Trail contact: Boulder Ranger District; (303) 541-2500; www.fs.usda.gov/recarea/arp/recarea/?recid=28178

Maps: National Geographic Trails Illustrated #102: Indian Peaks/Gold Hill
Nearest town: Jamestown
Cell service: None at trail or in the canyon on the drive up
Special considerations: No camping allowed within 0.25 mile of South St. Vrain Creek. Moose and bears are active in the area. Read the signage at the trailhead to learn more about what to do in the unlikely event that you encounter one of these animals. Afternoon thunderstorms are common in this area, so try to hike early if possible. This easily accessible hike can get very busy on the weekends during the summer, so while there are approximately 30 parking spots in the lot, get there early during the peak months.

Finding the trailhead: From the intersection of Boulder Canyon Drive (CO 119) and US 36 in Boulder, drive north for 3.5 miles. Turn left on Lee Hill Drive for 1.6 miles. When Lee Hill Drive bears left, continue straight onto Olde Stage Road. After 3.1 miles, turn left onto Lefthand Canyon Drive. This road will turn into James Canyon Drive just before Jamestown and Overland Road after you pass through Jamestown. Follow the road for 10.5 miles. Turn right on Riverside Lane to the trailhead parking lot. GPS: N40 07.46' / W105 26.55'

The Hike

The Ceran St. Vrain Trail leads you through a lodgepole pine forest sprinkled with wildflowers—all with the sounds of rushing water in the background. It's a fantastic option for families or for a picnic, and is popular with campers and anglers as well.

The trail is named after Ceran St. Vrain, a fur trader and fort builder. Born in St. Louis, he came to Colorado in 1824 for the fur trade, then established several forts on the plains with his business partner Charles Bent from 1830 until 1840. One of

The trail follows South St. Vrain Creek until it connects with FR 252.

the most famous is Fort St. Vrain at the confluence of South St. Vrain Creek and the South Platte River. Ceran St. Vrain is regarded as one of the leading pioneers in the West.

The number of other hikers starts thinning out considerably after you cross the bridge and start moving away from the trailhead. There are many little spur trails that go down to the water; at 0.4 mile, follow the trail to the left to go uphill and overlook the creek.

At 1.9 miles, you'll reach the intersection with FR 252. Go straight and at 2.1 miles, turn left to start a difficult climb. The grade is as much as 20 percent in some spots here, so be especially careful on your way back down. At 2.8 miles, the grade eases up and you'll turn right to continue on to FR 252A. The massive Miller Rock will start to peek out between the trees and come into view on your left at around 3 miles. Go past the rock and then around, and/or scramble up for the easier route and the best views.

When you're ready to leave, continue past Miller Rock to finish the lollipop loop. Right before 3.2 miles, stay on the higher trail on the left; it looks like the trail goes to the right and down, but I can assure you it does not. At 3.3 miles, you'll turn right

The tree cover makes this hike a great option for a warmer day.

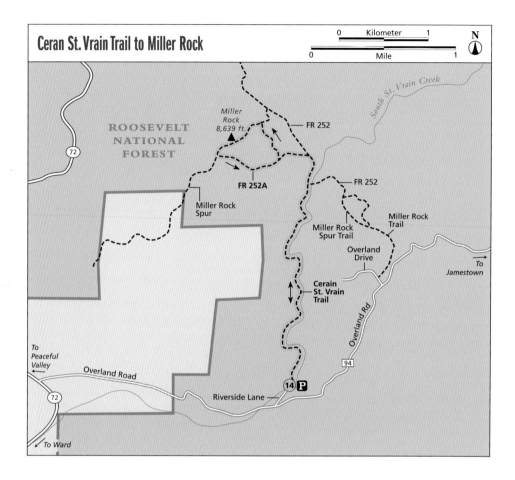

Ceran St. Vrain Trail to Miller Rock

to continue downhill. There may be a few downed trees along the trail at this point, but they're easy enough to maneuver over or around. At 3.7 miles, you'll reconnect with the main trail. Take a left and head down the steep slope.

Turn right at 4 miles and then stay right and high at 4.2 miles to reconnect with the Ceran St. Vrain Trail back to the trailhead.

Miles and Directions

0.0 Start at the Ceran St. Vrain Trailhead and go over the bridge.

0.3 Cross a creek that cuts across the trail.

0.4 Follow the trail left and uphill.

1.9 Stay straight onto FR 252.

2.1 Turn left and start a steep climb.

2.8 Turn right onto FR 252A.

3.0 Arrive at Miller Rock.

On many of the hikes in this guide, you'll notice different kinds of pine trees. Along this trail, you'll see some of them side by side. In the images below, you'll see spruce trees have sharp, square needles (right), while pine needles are prickly—lodgepole pines have two needles in each packet (left).

3.2 Stay on the higher trail to the left.

3.3 Turn right to stay on the loop.

3.7 Turn left.

4.0 Turn right.

4.2 Stay right and high to reconnect with the Ceran St. Vrain Trail.

6.0 Arrive back at the trailhead.

Additional Route Options

For an easy family adventure that comes in just under 4 miles, turn around at FR 252.

15 Crater Lakes via South Boulder Creek Trail

This challenging trail showcases some of the best of the James Peak Wilderness. You'll walk through the forest along South Boulder Creek, get gorgeous mountain views, and experience three alpine lakes—all while getting in a solid workout.

Start: East Portal Trailhead
Distance: 6.8 miles out and back
Difficulty: Strenuous
Elevation gain: 1,853 feet
Hiking time: 2-3 hours
Trail surface: Dirt with some rocky spots
Seasons/schedule: Mid- to late summer
Fees and permits: None
Other trail users: None
Canine compatibility: Dogs must be on leash at all times.
Land status: James Peak Wilderness

Trail contact: Boulder Ranger District; (303) 541-2500; www.fs.usda.gov/recarea/arp/recarea/?recid=28178
Maps: National Geographic Trails Illustrated #103: Winter Park/Central City/Rollins Pass
Nearest town: Nederland (Rollinsville doesn't have many services)
Cell service: None
Special considerations: Groups are limited to 12 people or fewer. The road to the trailhead is dirt and can be a little bumpy, but is accessible for most cars.

Finding the trailhead: From the intersection of Boulder Canyon Drive (CO 119) and Broadway (CO 93) in Boulder, drive west on CO 119 for 16 miles. At the traffic circle in Nederland, take the third exit to stay on CO 119 (North Bridge Street) for 4.8 miles. Turn right onto Tolland Road/East Portal Road. Follow the dirt road for 8.1 miles to a dead end at the trailhead. GPS: N39 55.44' / W105 14.13'

The Hike

The moment you pull up to the trailhead, you'll notice the huge Moffat train and water tunnel. The first train ran through here in February 1928, and about fifteen trains still use the tunnel to deliver part of Denver's water supply as well as transport people on Amtrak's California Zephyr train. Named after railroad pioneer David Moffat, the Moffat Tunnel gave Denver a direct western route through the Continental Divide. The West Portal is near Winter Park Ski Resort, and the East Portal is a trailhead for a handful of hikes in the James Peak Wilderness.

To get to Crater Lakes, start along the South Boulder Creek Trail in the northwest part of the parking lot. There's some gradual climbing, but this is the perfect time to enjoy the scenery

In June and even into July, there can still be deep snow on the Crater Lakes Trail, making the switchbacks a bit difficult to follow. Look for the cairns marking the trail or save this one for late summer/early fall.

The three Crater Lakes sit just below the Continental Divide, the western boundary of the Front Range.

Snow can stick around this forested area until June or even July.

and the occasional view through the trees. In 1.2 miles, go straight at the junction with the Forest Lakes Trail (there's a sign). Just before 2 miles, you'll come to another intersection: the South Boulder Creek Trail will take a left and you'll go right to get on the Crater Lakes Trail. (***Note:*** As of September 2023, the sign here was broken, so be careful not to miss this junction.) This is where the challenging part of the trail comes in.

Follow the rocky switchbacks up for a mile until the trail levels out at the lower lakes. Once you've spent some time here, continue on the path between Lower Crater Lake South and Lower Crater Lake North along Crater Lakes Creek to Upper Crater Lake, sitting at 11,000 feet in the shadow of the Continental Divide.

Crater Lakes via South Boulder Creek Trail

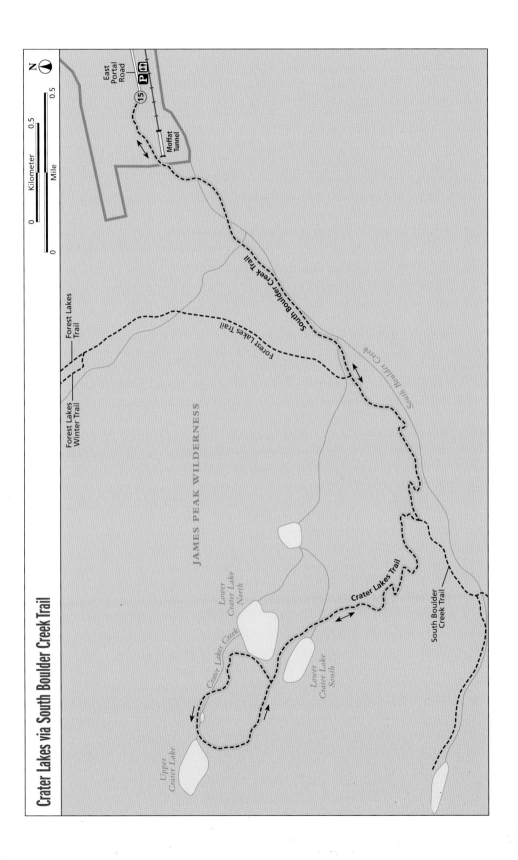

East Portal Road

15

Moffat Tunnel

Forest Lakes Trail

Forest Lakes Winter Trail

Forest Lakes Trail

South Boulder Creek Trail

Forest Lakes Trail

South Boulder Creek

JAMES PEAK WILDERNESS

Crater Lakes Creek

Lower Crater Lake North

Lower Crater Lake South

Crater Lakes Trail

South Boulder Creek Trail

Upper Crater Lake

N

Kilometer

0   0.5

0   0.5

Mile

The creek (and the trail) creates a loop with the upper lake feeding into the lower lakes, so you can go clockwise or counterclockwise. Follow the trail back down and to the parking lot.

Miles and Directions

0.0 From the East Portal Trailhead, take the northwest route on the South Boulder Creek Trail.

1.2 Come to a junction with the Forest Lakes Trail; go straight.

1.9 Come to a junction with the Crater Lakes Trail; turn right and head up the switchbacks.

2.7 Arrive at the Lower Crater Lakes.

2.9 The trail splits to go up to Upper Crater Lake; take either direction.

3.4 Arrive at Upper Crater Lake.

3.9 Complete the loop and meet back with the Crater Lakes Trail.

4.9 Turn left onto the South Boulder Creek Trail.

6.8 Arrive back at the trailhead.

Additional Route Options

For more miles and an added challenge, take the South Boulder Creek Trail where it splits off of the Crater Lakes Trail and hike to Rogers Pass Lake (2.1 miles one way) and then Heart Lake (2.6 miles one way). Another option is to take the South Boulder Creek Trail for 0.3 mile, then turn right on the Clayton Lake Trail for 0.6 mile. Return the way you came for either option.

16 Rattlesnake Gulch Trail–Eldorado Canyon State Park

Eldorado Canyon State Park is well known in the climbing world for its incredible routes, and while the hiking trails are fewer than the climbs, they're pretty good too. Rattlesnake Gulch offers impressive views of the canyon (no climbing shoes required!), takes you by the Crags Hotel ruin, and finishes with a wonderful vista of the Continental Divide.

Start: Rattlesnake Gulch and Fowler Trailhead
Distance: 3.8-mile lollipop (3 miles out and back if loop is closed)
Difficulty: Moderately strenuous
Elevation gain: 1,000 feet
Hiking time: 1-2 hours
Trail surface: Dirt and rocks
Seasons/schedule: Year-round; best spring through fall. The park is open from sunrise to sunset.
Fees and permits: Daily entrance fee or annual state parks pass required
Other trail users: Mountain bikers
Canine compatibility: Dogs allowed on leash
Land status: Eldorado Canyon State Park
Trail contact: Eldorado Canyon State Park; (303) 494-3943; https://cpw.state.co.us/placestogo/parks/EldoradoCanyon

Maps: Eldorado Canyon State Park map
Nearest town: Superior (no services in Eldorado Springs)
Cell service: Spotty
Special considerations: A timed reservation is required to enter the park on weekends and holidays between May 15 and September 15. Reservations are limited, but there is also a shuttle system (you also need a reservation for this). The reservation is in addition to the daily entrance fee. Learn more at https://cpw.state.co.us/placestogo/parks/Eldorado Canyon/Pages/vehiclereservations.aspx. If the parking lot is full on a non-reservation day, you will be turned away. There are no other parking options nearby.

Finding the trailhead: From the intersection of Table Mesa Drive and Broadway (CO 93) in Boulder, drive south on CO 93 for 2.5 miles. Turn right onto Eldorado Springs Drive (CO 170) and drive 3.1 miles into Eldorado Springs. Go past the swimming pool and turn left into Eldorado Canyon State Park. The trailhead is 0.5 mile down the narrow dirt road. There will be a small parking area on your left. If that lot is full, the next closest lot is at the visitor center, which is 0.3 mile farther down the road. Do not park in the pullouts on the side of the road; those are for passing. GPS: N39 55.77' / W105 17.41'

The Hike

Today, Eldorado Springs is a quiet little artist enclave, but in the early 1900s it was a bustling resort town with a dancing hall, roller-skating rink, pool hall, and arcade (before then, the Ute frequented the canyon's warm springs for health and spiritual renewal). The Grandview Rooming House and the New Eldorado Hotel were

This hike includes some fantastic views, like this one out of the canyon and toward the plains.

packed every weekend, and A. D. Stencel purchased 40 acres of Eldorado Canyon for the Crags Hotel. After taking the train from Denver, visitors could hike up the trail by foot or via horse-drawn buggy to the accommodations overlooking the canyon. Part of the Rattlesnake Gulch Trail follows this route, which was once known as Crags Boulevard. In November 1912, the hotel burned to the ground, and all that's left are some crumbled rock walls, the courtyard fountain, and a stone fireplace.

Starting at the Rattlesnake Gulch and Fowler Trailhead, head up a short rocky uphill through the ponderosa pine and juniper forest. Around 0.25 mile, the trail widens and gets steeper again, but there are plenty of views to look at as you make your way up.

At 1.3 miles, you'll come to an intersection with the Crags Hotel ruins on your right, the Rattlesnake Gulch Trail straight ahead, and the Rattlesnake Gulch Loop to your left. I suggest following the loop, but depending on when you hike here, that section may be closed until as late as July to protect nesting golden

In Spanish, *el dorado* means "gilded" or "covered with gold." Colorado Parks & Wildlife says this may refer to the golden lichen on the cliffs, but if you go down to the stream and the sun hits the sand beneath the water just right, it will sparkle with a bright gold color.

Rattlesnake Gulch Trail—Eldorado Canyon State Park

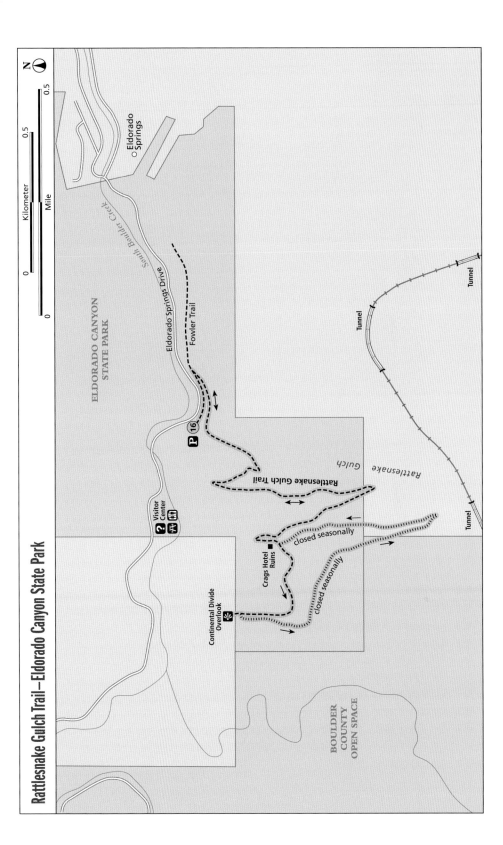

The trail winds through the forest, with canyon views peeking through from time to time.

eagles. There will be a sign indicating if the trail is closed. If you're able to take the loop, you'll have even better views to the east and you'll see the old access trail to the railroad tracks for people who arrived at the Crags Hotel by train. Continue straight after the Crags Hotel ruins to the Continental Divide Overlook.

To return to the trailhead, either finish the loop or backtrack the way you came if you skipped the loop.

Miles and Directions

- **0.0** Start at the Rattlesnake Gulch and Fowler Trailhead.
- **0.1** Come to the junction of the two trails; turn right onto the Rattlesnake Gulch Trail.
- **0.4** Turn right and cross a long bridge.
- **1.3** Arrive at the intersection with the Crags Hotel ruins on your right, the Rattlesnake Gulch Trail straight ahead, and the Rattlesnake Gulch Loop to your left. Explore the ruins and then take the loop.
- **1.7** Continue right up the switchback.
- **2.1** Stay to the right.
- **2.2** Turn right to go 0.1 mile out to the Continental Divide Overlook. Finish the loop before returning to the trailhead. If the loop is closed, backtrack the way you came for a 3-mile hike.
- **3.8** Arrive back at the trailhead.

17 Flatirons Vista Trail

The Flatirons Vista Trail offers an array of wildflowers in the spring and sweeping views of the iconic Flatirons. This easy hike is great for a family outing, an adventure with the pups, or a quick lap for trail runners before dusk in the summer.

Start: Flatirons Vista Trailhead
Distance: 3.4-mile loop
Difficulty: Easy
Elevation gain: 285 feet
Hiking time: 1–1.5 hours
Trail surface: Dirt with some rocky spots
Seasons/schedule: Year-round; best spring through fall. Trail closes when conditions are too muddy.
Fees and permits: Fee for vehicles not registered in Boulder County
Other trail users: Equestrians and mountain bikers
Canine compatibility: Dogs must be on leash at all times unless they meet Boulder's voice and sight control standard and display a City of Boulder Voice and Sight tag.
Land status: Boulder Open Space and Mountain Parks
Trail contact: Boulder County Parks and Open Space; (303) 541-2500; www.bouldercounty .gov/departments/parks-and-open-space
Maps: OSMP Trail Map
Nearest town: Superior
Cell service: Spotty
Special considerations: If the parking lot is full, you'll have to come back—do not park along CO 93. The trail may be closed due to mud or weather conditions.

Finding the trailhead: From the intersection of Boulder Canyon Drive (CO 119) and Broadway (CO 93) in Boulder, drive south on CO 93 for 7.4 miles. Turn into the parking area on your right. It's easy to spot, as there is nothing else in the area except the well-established parking lot with restrooms. GPS: N39 55.44' / W105 14.13'

The Hike

While this trail is accessible year-round, mild temperatures and the wildflower bloom make spring a wonderful time to try this hike. It's one of the best places to see wildflowers in and around Boulder.

From the parking lot, go through the gate (don't forget to close it behind you!) and follow the wide dirt path in a counterclockwise direction to maximize the vistas this trail is named after. Less than 0.1 mile in, stay to the left as the trail winds toward the mountains. (Many mountain bikers use this Greenbelt Connector trail to hop on Flatirons Vista from the Greenbelt Plateau Trailhead.) Walk up a gentle hill for the first 1.2 miles, passing the prairie grassland and soaking in expansive views of Boulder's famous Flatirons.

> Keep an eye overhead for various songbirds in the spring and golden and bald eagles in the winter.

The beginning of the hike has the best views of Boulder's Flatirons.

Once you get to the top of the mesa, Flatirons Vista North connects to the Doudy Draw Trail and turns into Flatirons Vista South. The intersection is marked, and you'll take a left onto Flatirons Vista South. The trail isn't as wide here, but is still comfortable for two people to walk side by side. As you venture into the ponderosa pine forest, be sure to look west to see mountains peeking between the trees.

As you come around and follow the fence line back toward the starting point, you will have a choice at 2.6 miles: return via Prairie Vista (0.9 mile) or stay on Flatirons Vista South (0.8 mile). Prairie Vista stays higher and offers more wildflowers, while Flatirons Vista South drops down and around the pond, where you can often see free-range cows drinking water.

Regardless of which option you take, the final 0.1 mile is on the Prairie Vista Trail and back to the parking lot.

Wildflowers like the hairyseed bahia are abundant throughout this hike.

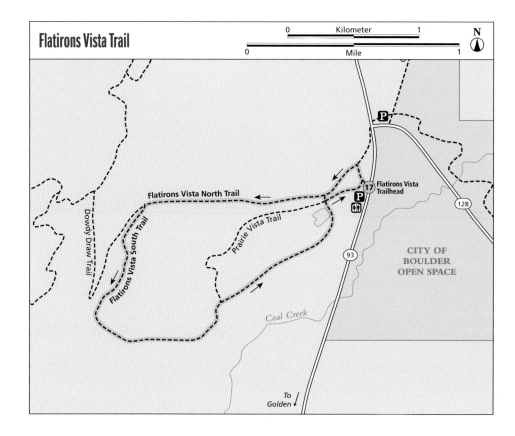

Flatirons Vista Trail

Miles and Directions

0.0 From the Flatirons Vista Trailhead, walk through the gate (be sure to close it behind you!) and turn right (north).

0.1 Bear left to stay on the Flatirons Vista North Trail.

0.3 Continue right to stay on Flatirons Vista North.

1.2 Take the left fork to the Flatirons Vista South Trail.

2.6 Come to an intersection with the Prairie Vista Trail; stay to the right.

3.3 Connect with the Prairie Vista Trail and head straight back to the parking lot.

3.4 Arrive back at the trailhead.

Additional Route Options

A popular connection here is to Doudy Draw, which will add approximately 3.3 miles to the hike. Take the Doudy Draw Trail to the Doudy Draw Trailhead and back to the connection with Flatirons Vista.

Bonus Hikes at a Glance

C. Green Mountain via Gregory Canyon and Ranger Trails

This 5.4-mile out-and-back hike is a challenging option just outside the heart of Boulder. Starting at the end of Gregory Canyon Road off Flagstaff Road, you'll climb 2,378 feet in 2.7 miles to the top of Green Mountain. The good news is that most of this hike is shaded and you'll be serenaded by songbirds most of the way. Once you get to the top, there are views of Boulder to the east and a brass marker that shows the peaks that you can see in the distance to the west.

The trail is fairly easy to follow. You'll pass two trail junctions in the first 0.3 mile; go straight through both. At 1.4 miles, Gregory Canyon Ts into the Ranger Trail; turn left and start climbing. There are some steep sections here. Continue straight through the trail junction at 1.6 miles, then turn right to stay on the Ranger Trail at 1.9 miles. Keep climbing! (At one point, the grade is more than 30 percent.) You'll reach the top at 2.7 miles. From here, you can retrace your steps or continue on the E. M. Greenman Trail down to the Saddle Rock Trail and back to the trailhead. Parking can get

At the top of Green Mountain, line up the peaks you see in the distance with the map.
Jacob Preble

busy in the summer (especially on weekends!), but there are also spots along Baseline Road. Nonresidents must pay for parking at the Green Mountain Trailhead, and a fee is required to park along Baseline. Dogs are allowed on leash.

Finding the trailhead: From the intersection of Baseline Road and Broadway (CO 93) in Boulder, drive west on Baseline Road for 1.4 miles. Turn left onto Gregory Canyon Road. The parking lot is at the end of the road. GPS: N39 59.85' / W105 17.57'

D. Lost Lake via Hessie Trail

Lost Lake is an incredible hike near Nederland, but it's also very popular so you may need to take advantage of the free shuttle during the summer (learn more at www.bouldercounty.gov/open-space/parks-and-trails/hessie-trailhead). Lost Lake is the perfect place for a summer picnic or a fall hike among the aspens. It's a 4-mile out-and-back hike to the lake, surrounded by the Indian Peaks. Walk past the old Hessie townsite and after 0.5 mile, cross the Happy Valley Bridge over the North Fork of Middle Boulder Creek. At the junction, you can go right or straight—both ways come back around to the trail just before 0.9 mile. Follow a steep and rocky old mining road and at 1.2 miles, turn left and cross the Lost Bridge. After passing a waterfall, you'll take a left at 1.5 miles and start a steep ascent to the lake. Return the way you came.

Finding the trailhead: From the intersection of Boulder Canyon Drive (CO 119) and Broadway (CO 93) in Boulder, drive west on CO 119 for 16 miles. At the traffic circle in Nederland, take the third exit to stay on CO 119 (North Bridge Street) for 0.6 mile. Turn right onto Eldora Road for 4.8 miles. Continue straight onto Hessie Road and the trailhead will be on your left in about 500 feet. Follow the dirt road for 8.1 miles to a dead end at the trailhead. GPS: N39 57.09' / W105 35.70'

Denver Area

L ike many cities and towns in the West, people originally came to Denver in search of gold. The first permanent settlements came in 1858—Auraria on the west side of Cherry Creek, Denver City on the east, and Highland on the bluffs to the north—and in 1861 the city of Denver became formally incorporated. It became the capital six years later. The city's role in a transcontinental

Get a fantastic view of the Denver skyline with the Front Range behind it from the Denver Museum of Nature & Science.

railroad ensured that it would stay relevant, and though people are no longer flocking out West in search of gold and other minerals, Denver is well known for its plethora of outdoor adventures.

The Mile High City is home to Colorado's only major (and international) airport and offers easy access to the mountains via I-70, so it only makes sense that many people use Denver as a launching point for everything from skiing and snowshoeing to hiking and climbing. It's become so popular that millions of people decided to move here, with the population in and around the Mile High City booming from 2011 to 2019. Population growth has slowed down since then for a variety of reasons, but the city is still in a prime location for anyone looking to do just about anything outside.

A good number of the hikes in this book are found in the greater Denver area, and that's only scratching the surface of what's out there. From an easy walk close to town to summiting one of the state's 14ers (peaks that reach over 14,000 feet in elevation), there are thousands of miles to be explored within an hour(ish)'s drive of Denver. This list isn't intended to be all-encompassing, but rather meant to give you a taste of what's out there and inspire you to explore even more.

18 Barr Lake Loop–Barr Lake State Park

Barr Lake is a quieter state park than many of the others in the state. Sitting northeast of Denver, there is a single dirt and gravel path that loops around the lake, through the habitats of the more than 350 species of birds that live here, including the bald eagle. The lake is also home to channel catfish, small and largemouth bass, rainbow trout, walleye, bluegill, wiper, and tiger muskie (a fishing license may be required).

Start: Nature Center
Distance: 8.8-mile loop
Difficulty: Easy
Elevation gain: 98 feet
Hiking time: 2.5–3.5 hours
Trail surface: Dirt
Seasons/schedule: Year-round. The park is open from 5 a.m. to 10 p.m. but fishing is allowed all night.
Fees and permits: Daily entrance fee or annual state parks pass required
Other trail users: Equestrians and mountain bikers
Canine compatibility: Dogs are allowed on-leash on part of this trail but not in the wildlife refuge portion, so you may want to leave them home for this one if you plan to do the full loop.

Land status: Barr Lake State Park; 659-6005; https://cpw.state.co.us/placestogo/parks/barrlake
Maps: Barr Lake State Park map
Nearest town: Brighton
Cell service: Good
Special considerations: Parts of this trail are closed seasonally, so check the website or stop by the Nature Center before you set out on the trail. The best time to see bald eagles is in the winter. Stay on designated trails. There is no swimming in the lake, but sailboats, hand-propelled craft, and boats with electric trolling motors or gasoline motors with 10 horsepower or less are allowed on the lake.

Finding the trailhead: From the intersection of I-25 and I-76 in Denver, drive east on I-76 for 16.5 miles. Take exit 22 for Bromley Lane and turn right. Continue onto East 152nd Avenue for 0.8 mile. Turn right onto Picadilly Road and continue for 1.9 miles, then turn right into Barr Lake State Park. Follow the park road for 1.1 miles to the Nature Center parking lot. GPS: N39 56.26' / W104 45.10'

The Hike

The lake you see before you is a prairie reservoir stretching across nearly 2,000 acres. In the late 1880s, Barr Lake was a thriving fishing area, but pollution almost destroyed it until laws and controls were put into place in the 1960s. Now, the land around the lake is filled with cottonwoods, aquatic plants, and marshes and the southern half of the lake is a designated wildlife refuge with a concentration and variety of birds that you won't find anywhere else in the state. The Nature Center is a great place to start and learn more about the wildlife you'll potentially see on your walk, like pelicans, great blue herons, cormorants, egrets, ducks, grebes, owls, eagles, and hawks. The large

This easy loop around Barr Lake offers views of the Front Range in the distance.

window in the back of the Nature Center is a great spot to quietly watch for birds around the feeders outside.

Start your walk at the obvious trail to the right of the Nature Center. Cross the bridge and turn left. The Niedrach Nature Trail takes you between a canal and the lake to a boardwalk on your right. On the boardwalk you'll find binoculars to give you a better look into the trees to the south, where you may see a bald eagle nest in the winter.

After you walk along the boardwalk and get back to the main trail, it will curve to the west to follow the lake. At the southwest end of the lake, there is another board-walk for the Rookery Gazebo. Open seasonally, this offers great views of the rookery and nests that sit high in the trees. Continue as the trail heads north and runs near the railroad tracks for 2.5 miles. Many people go to the end of the trees and turn around instead of taking this path by the subdivision, but it will give you a different perspective of the park if you decide to continue.

When you reach the north end of the lake, follow the trail to the right and over the dam. This part of the trail is closed during waterfowl hunting days (Wednesdays and Saturdays from October through February). When you turn right to head back

Barr Lake Loop–Barr Lake State Park

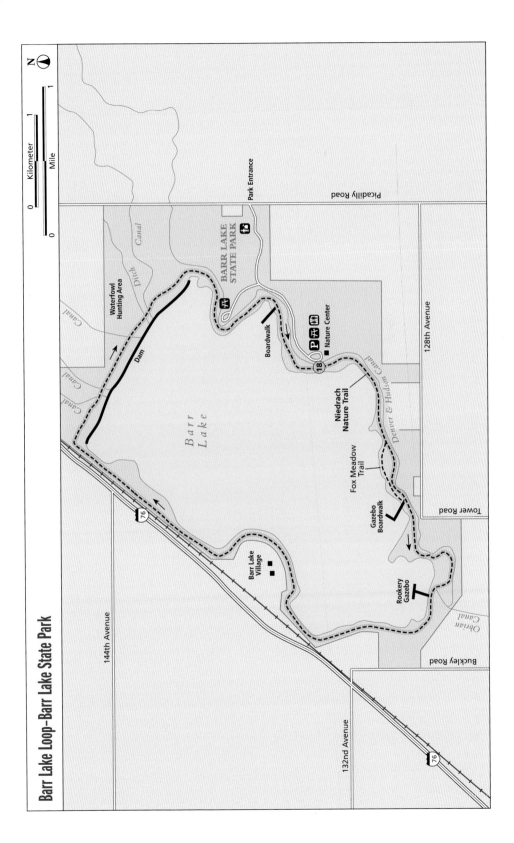

A bald eagle nest as seen through the binoculars on the Gazebo Boardwalk.

to your starting point, you'll walk through the wildlife area and by a fishing pier and boat launch. Finish your walk back at the trailhead by the Nature Center.

Miles and Directions

0.0   Start at the trailhead by the Nature Center. Cross the bridge and turn left.

1.4   Arrive at the Gazebo Boardwalk.

2.5   Arrive at the Rookery Gazebo.

6.7   Arrive at the dam.

8.8   Arrive back at the trailhead.

19 Raccoon Trail–Golden Gate Canyon State Park

Golden Gate Canyon State Park is one of my favorite places to hike in Colorado. There's almost 35 miles of hiking trails across 12,000 acres and elevations ranging from 7,600 to 10,400 feet. Each of the eleven trails are named after animals native to the area. The Raccoon Trail is a moderate loop through open meadows and aspen groves, with a stop at Panorama Point.

Start: Reverend's Ridge Campground
Distance: 3.6-mile lollipop
Difficulty: Moderate
Elevation gain: 679 feet
Hiking time: 1–2 hours
Trail surface: Dirt with some rocky spots
Seasons/schedule: Spring through fall. The park is open from 5 a.m. to 10 p.m.
Fees and permits: Daily entrance fee or annual state parks pass required
Other trail users: Equestrians and mountain bikers
Canine compatibility: Dogs must be on leash at all times.
Land status: Golden Gate Canyon State Park

Trail contact: Golden Gate Canyon State Park; (303) 582-3707; https://cpw.state.co.us/placestogo/parks/GoldenGateCanyon
Maps: Golden Gate Canyon State Park map
Nearest town: Central City/Blackhawk
Cell service: None
Special considerations: There is limited parking at the campground, especially on weekends in the summer. A park ranger is often there counting spots, so ask about parking on Gap Road. If no spots are available, you could also start this hike at Panorama Point. There is a small, seasonal visitor center at the campground as well as a self-service pay station.

Finding the trailhead: From the intersection of I-25 and I-70 in Denver, drive west on I-70 for 8.5 miles. Take exit 265 for CO 58 toward Golden/Central City and continue for 5.4 miles, then turn right onto CO 93 for 1.4 miles. Turn left onto CO 46 (Golden Gate Canyon Boulevard) and follow this road for 12.7 miles. Turn right onto Crawford Gulch Road to the park's visitor center, if you'd like. From there, backtrack to continue on CO 46 for 1.3 miles. Turn right onto Mountain Base Road and drive 3.2 miles. Turn left on Gap Road and then take an immediate right onto State Park Road. In 0.4 mile, you'll reach Reverend's Ridge Campground. GPS: N39 52.56' / W105 26.94'

The Hike

Like many parks and open spaces in the Front Range, Golden Gate Canyon State Park started as a homestead for former miners like John Frazer and Hugh McCammon. Some original buildings are still standing in the park, like Bootlegger's Cabin (along the Coyote Trail), from the days of distillation of illegal whiskey during Prohibition. The area became Colorado's second state park in 1960.

The view from Panorama Point is pretty no matter what the season.

The trail starts just beyond the small, seasonal visitor center and self-pay station. Start to the left and downhill. Go right at the split at 0.2 mile (it's just another trail from the campground that leads to the Raccoon Trail). Most of this hike is in the trees, making it a good option if you're looking to get outside on a windy day. (It also makes the hike especially beautiful in the fall when the aspens are changing!) The loop starts at 0.5 mile. Turn left to go clockwise around the loop. At just over 0.6 mile, turn right to stay on the Raccoon Trail and follow the rolling hills.

Stay right at 1.6 miles, when the Raccoon Trail joins with the Mule Deer Trail and both go toward Panorama Point. You'll reach Panorama Point at 2 miles, where you'll find restrooms, picnic tables, and a viewing deck. It's worth a stop to take in the views of the Rockies, including Mount Blue Sky (formerly Mount Evans) and Longs Peak. By the steps, you'll see where the trail goes down and around on both sides to continue on the Raccoon/Mule Deer Trail. At 2.6 miles, the trails split and you'll go right to stay on the Raccoon Trail. Finish the loop at 3 miles and turn left to head back to the campground.

There are several stands of aspens along the trail. If you come at the right time in the fall, these trees are filled with bright yellow and orange leaves that flutter in the breeze.

Raccoon Trail—Golden Gate Canyon State Park

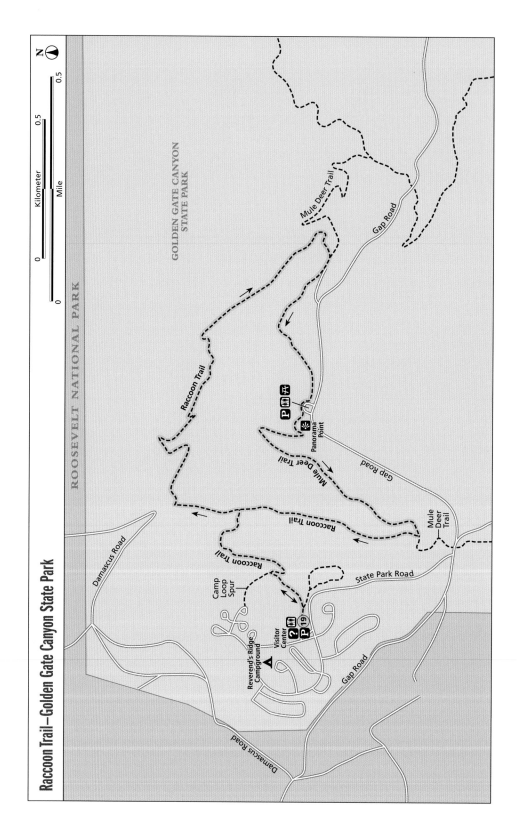

The aspens you'll see on the trail are not individual trees, like other species. Many aspen groves are not individual trees but are clonal colonies connected by a shared root system. Colonies can be thousands of years old, making them among the oldest living organisms on Earth. They also grow quickly—up to 2 feet per year—and Indigenous people used various parts of the tree for medicinal, ceremonial, and practical purposes like baskets.

Miles and Directions

0.0 From the campground, walk around the visitor center and self-service pay station and follow the trail to the left.

0.2 Turn right.

0.5 Start the loop by going clockwise (left).

0.6 Turn right.

1.6 Stay right when the trail converges with the Mule Deer Trail.

2.0 Arrive at Panorama Point.

2.6 Go right.

3.0 Turn left to return to the campground.

3.6 Arrive back at the trailhead.

Additional Route Options

There are plenty of ways to increase your mileage in this trail system. Mule Deer is a 9.1-mile loop that you can add on and connect to many of the other trails in the park for a full-day hike. There are two campgrounds (Reverend's Ridge and Aspen Meadow) plus backcountry campsites if you'd like to make it a weekend adventure or longer.

20 Beaver Brook and Chavez Trail Loop

The Beaver Brook Trail is no walk in the park, dropping down to Beaver Brook before climbing out of the gulch and heading back on the Chavez Trail. There is some rock scrambling involved and a creek crossing or two, but that's all part of the fun!

Start: Genesee Park Trailhead
Distance: 5-mile lollipop
Difficulty: Strenuous
Elevation gain: 1,109 feet
Hiking time: 2-3.5 hours
Trail surface: Dirt and rock
Seasons/schedule: Year-round; best spring through fall. The trailhead is open 1 hour before sunrise to 1 hour after sunset.
Fees and permits: None
Other trail users: None
Canine compatibility: Dogs must be on leash at all times.
Land status: Denver Mountain Park System

Trail contact: Denver Mountain Park System; (720) 913-1311; www.denvergov.org/Community/Parks-and-Public-Spaces/Parks-Directory/Genesee-Park
Maps: National Geographic Trails Illustrated #100: Boulder/Golden
Nearest town: Golden or Morrison
Cell service: At trailhead but not on trail
Special considerations: There is a good number of parking spots at the trailhead, but they may fill up quickly during busy summer weekends. Some parking is available along the road. Parts of the trail along the brook at the bottom may be flooded after a lot of rain.

Finding the trailhead: From the intersection of US 6 and I-25 in Denver, drive west on US 6 for 8.8 miles. Take the exit onto I-70 toward Grand Junction and continue on I-70 for 8.6 miles. Take exit 253 toward Chief Hosa. At the bottom of the exit, turn right and then immediately right onto Stapleton Road. Follow Stapleton Road for 0.8 mile and turn left into the trailhead parking lot. GPS: N39 43.02' / W105 18.93'

The Hike

From the parking lot, start walking through the trees along the Beaver Brook Trail. It starts out easy, with the sun shining through the trees and purple aspen daisies lining the trail. At 0.4 mile, stay straight on the Beaver Brook Trail. Stay straight again at 1 mile (the other route is clearly blocked, so you can't miss it).

At 1.8 miles, Beaver Brook starts as a trickle on the right side of the trail as you head downhill. Don't worry—it gets more impressive! The trickle will cross back and forth over the trail several times as you make your way down. When you get to the main bridge that crosses the brook, the trail turns right, but if you take a little detour to the left, you'll see some small cascades and a nice little area for a break.

As you wind your way through the gulch, there are more bridges and some scrambling over smoothly worn rocks. Take your time and be careful through here. At 2.5 miles, the trail goes straight but there is a sign indicating an alternate route to the left over a log if the water ahead is too high.

You'll start to see Beaver Brook as a trickle along the trail, but by the time you get to the bottom of the gulch, it's a full-flowing waterway.

At 2.7 miles, you'll have to climb over some rocks. Follow the water and then go around the biggest rock on the left-hand side for an easier route. Once you cross the bridge and start to come up away from the brook, the Chavez Trail connects with Beaver Brook. This junction is at about 2.9 miles, and you almost have to turn all the way around to see the trail. A sign tells you to turn around/take a right, but there's no cell service, so make sure you are tracking your mileage with a GPS so you don't miss the turn or you'll be setting out for a 10-mile one-way trek.

There are some rock steps and a narrow section as you come out of the gulch. The incline varies from gradual to over 20 percent and really doesn't let up until you get back to the Beaver Brook Trail. At 4.3 miles, there is a lovely bench overlooking

The Colorado Mountain Club (CMC) completed the Beaver Brook Trail in 1919. In 1926, Alice Hale wrote in the May issue of the CMC's *Trail & Timberline* magazine that designing the Beaver Brook Trail "took time and thought . . . to make it the best way . . . with the finest views, with the spring just where it is needed, and the charming dips into the steep cool ravines coming as a sharp contrast to the long stretches on the very edge of the hills."

Aspen daisies are plentiful along the first part of the trail.

The hike winds through the trees and down the gulch to Beaver Brook before climbing back up.

the brook, and then you'll continue straight versus going left over the bridge. The signage shows both the left and straight trail as the Braille Trail, and both go back to the same point.

At 4.6 miles, you'll cross a large dirt road. Go across the road and look for a trail that veers off into the grasses on your right. Take that trail until you come back to the intersection with the Beaver Brook Trail. Hang a left and after a slight hill, it's an easy final walk back to the parking lot.

Miles and Directions

0.0 From the southeast area of the parking lot, start at the trailhead.

0.4 Stay straight to stay on Beaver Brook Trail.

1.0 Stay straight to stay on Beaver Brook Trail.

2.1 Go over the bridge and follow the trail to the right.

2.5 Go straight, or turn left to take the alternate route if the water is too high.

2.9 Cross bridge and make a sharp turn to the right to get on the Chavez Trail.

4.3 Stay straight to stay on the Chavez Trail.

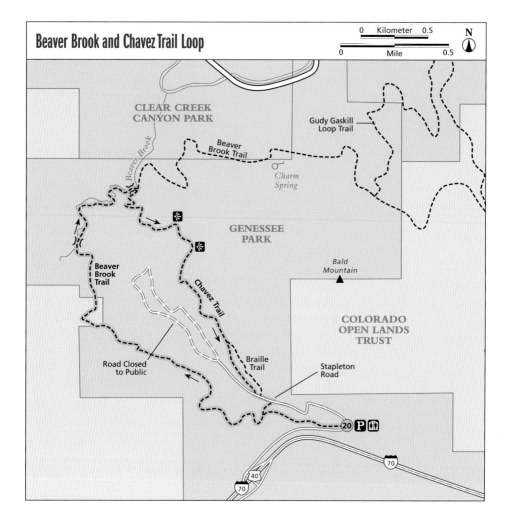

4.6 Cross the dirt road and bear right to stay on Chavez Trail.

4.7 Turn left to get back on the Beaver Brook Trail and return to the parking lot.

5.0 Arrive back at the parking lot.

Additional Route Options

The full Beaver Brook Trail is a 10-mile point-to-point route from Genesee Park to the East Trailhead in Windy Saddle Park. For even more mileage, stay on Beaver Brook instead of jumping on Chavez and at 4.3 miles, add on the 2.4-mile Gudy Gaskill Loop for an overlook of Clear Creek Canyon.

21 Mount Falcon Park Upper Loop

Mount Falcon Park offers an opportunity to both spend some time in nature and see a bit of the Front Range's history up close. Walk through open meadows where deer frequently graze (and wild turkeys have been spotted), check out the mountain views from the Eagle Eye Shelter, summit 7,841-foot Mount Falcon, and explore the Walker Home ruins before getting to the turnaround, where you'll see Red Rocks and the greater Denver area.

Start: Mount Falcon Park West Trailhead

Distance: 4.2 miles out and back with a loop in the middle

Difficulty: Easy-moderate

Elevation gain: 591 feet

Hiking time: 1.5–2 hours

Trail surface: Dirt

Seasons/schedule: Year-round; best spring through fall. The park is open 1 hour before sunrise to 1 hour after sunset.

Fees and permits: None

Other trail users: Mountain bikers

Canine compatibility: Dogs must be on leash at all times.

Land status: Jefferson County Open Space

Trail contact: Jeffco Open Space; (303) 271-5925; www.jeffco.us/1332/Mount-Falcon-Park

Maps: Mount Falcon Park map

Nearest town: Morrison

Cell service: Spotty

Special considerations: None

Finding the trailhead: From the intersection of US 6 and I-25 in Denver, drive west on US 6 for 8.8 miles. Take the exit onto I-70 toward Grand Junction and continue on I-70 for 1 mile. Use the right two lanes to take exit 260 for CO 470 toward Colorado Springs. Merge onto CO 470 and continue for 5.1 miles. Take exit 5A for US 285 toward Fairplay for 4.5 miles. Turn right onto Parmalee Gulch Road and continue for 2.7 miles. Turn right onto Picutis Road, then left onto Comanche Road. You'll see signs for Mount Falcon Park as you wind your way through the Indian Hills neighborhood. Turn right onto Ohkay Road, then right onto Picutis Road again. Go 0.4 mile, then keep left to continue onto Nambe Road for 0.6 mile. This turns into Mount Falcon Road. Follow this road for 0.6 mile to the West Trailhead parking lot. GPS: N39 38.17' / W105 14.29'

The Hike

The trail starts on the east side of the parking lot. There is an informational kiosk and restrooms 0.1 mile in. Follow the gradual uphill and stay to the right when the trail splits around 0.4 mile. Continue up until you see the Eagle Eye Shelter on your right, where you'll find covered picnic tables and a wonderful view of the Indian Hills and Continental Divide. From 1933 to 1972, the shelter was a summer cabin for the Kirchof family—not a bad spot, eh? The family built a well nearby and added the phrase "am Brunnen vor dem Tore" in iron above it. German for "at the Well before the Gate," you can listen to the song from which the words came at the interpretive sign in front of the shelter.

The trail winds through the forest and open meadows, with some fantastic views along the way, like this one from the Eagle Eye Shelter.

Continue on the path and stop by the lookout tower on the summit of Mount Falcon, surrounded by Douglas firs. Just after a mile, you'll connect with the Meadow Trail and walk through the meadow and up to the Walker Home ruins. Lightning struck the home and burned it down in 1918, but most of the foundation remains. Built by stonemasons from Italy, the mansion included ten bedrooms, a music room, an observation deck, eight fireplaces (including the one you can still see standing today), a library, and servants' quarters. If you walk around the ruins, you can see Red Rocks Amphitheatre in the distance. Imagine what the view from the observation deck must've been like!

John Brisben Walker was a self-made millionaire who preserved thousands of acres in the Morrison area, including Mount Falcon Park, named after the birds they saw circling overhead during a site visit. Walker was a staunch advocate for a system of mountain parks in Denver. He had a big vision for Denver, including concerts at Red Rocks and a summer White House for US presidents. Many of his dreams came true.

One of the eight original fireplaces from the Walker Home remains.

Deer can often be found grazing around sunset.

After exploring the ruins (you can walk around the area, but respect the signs that say to stay out of the actual homesite), go back to the main trail and continue east. (**Note:** This section may be closed if conditions are too muddy.) There's a picnic shelter just after 2 miles with some decent views of Denver. Keep going to Walker's Dream Trail and head to the top, where the trail comes to an end and you'll turn around. It's here that John Walker imagined a summer White House for US presidents, overlooking Denver.

On your way back, stay to the right after the ruins to follow the Castle Trail all the way back through the meadow and to the parking lot.

Mount Falcon Park Upper Loop

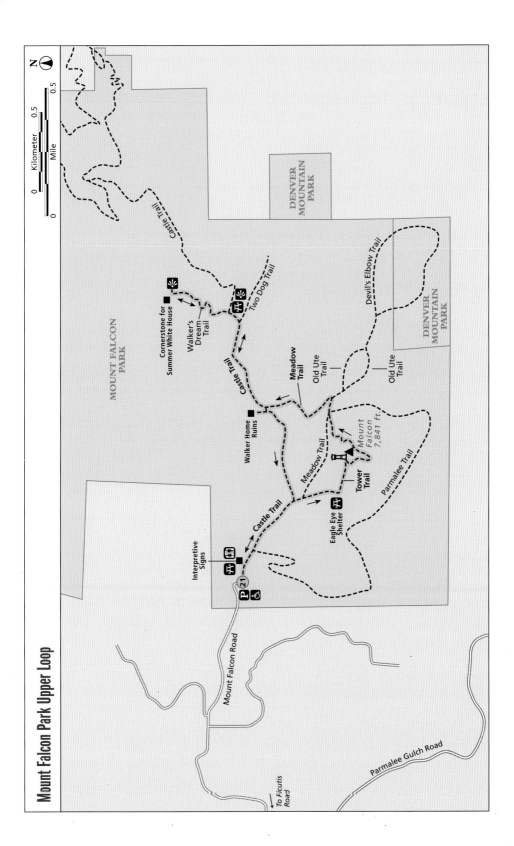

Miles and Directions

0.0 From the southeast area of the parking lot, start at the West Trailhead.

0.4 Bear right onto the Tower Trail.

0.6 Arrive at the Eagle Eye Shelter.

0.8 Arrive at the Mount Falcon summit.

1.2 Continue to the right on the Meadow Trail.

1.3 Make a sharp left to stay on the Meadow Trail.

1.6 Cross the Castle Trail and arrive at the Walker Home ruins. Go back to the Castle Trail and turn left.

2.1 At the intersection with the Two Dog Trail, stay to the left on the Castle Trail.

2.2 The Castle Trail turns right and goes downhill. Stay to the left onto Walker's Dream Trail.

2.6 Arrive at the end of the trail. Turn around and return the way you came.

3.4 Continue straight.

3.8 Turn right.

4.2 Arrive back at the trailhead.

Additional Route Options

For a shorter, 3.5-mile hike, skip the loop and go straight out and back on the Castle Trail to Walker's Dream Trail. For more of a challenge, add on the Old Ute Trail and the Devil's Elbow Trail loops by going right at 1.3 miles. These two loops add 2.5 miles.

22 Dakota Ridge Trail

Dakota Ridge isn't the quietest hike in this guide considering it runs on a ridge between two major highways, but it's still worth the trip. The challenging hike traverses the hogback 1,050 feet above the surrounding landscape to the famous dinosaur footprints on the southeast side.

Start: Matthews/Winters Park Trailhead
Distance: 4.9 miles out and back
Difficulty: Strenuous
Elevation gain: 1,050 feet
Hiking time: 2-3 hours
Trail surface: Mostly rocky
Seasons/schedule: Year-round. The park is open 1 hour before sunrise to 1 hour after sunset.
Fees and permits: None
Other trail users: Mountain bikers

Canine compatibility: Dogs must be on leash at all times.
Land status: Jefferson County Open Space
Trail contact: Jeffco Open Space; (303) 271-5925; www.jeffco.us/1292/ Matthews-Winter-Park
Maps: Matthews/Winters Park map
Nearest town: Golden
Cell service: Good
Special considerations: None

Finding the trailhead: From the intersection of US 6 and I-25 in Denver, drive west on US 6 for 8.8 miles. Take the exit onto I-70 toward Grand Junction and continue on I-70 for 2.2 miles. Take exit 5A for US 259 toward CR 93/Morrison. Turn left onto CR 93 for 0.2 mile and then left into the Stegosaurus Lot. There are many parking spots at this lot, and the trailhead is at the south end. GPS: N39 41.91' / W105 12.21'

The Hike

The trailhead is at the south end of the parking lot, and you'll immediately reverse directions and head up the steep and rocky hill to your left. About halfway up, take a sharp right at the gate; the incline eases up shortly after. Expect rolling hills with steep sections for most of this trail.

Just after 0.5 mile, take a break at the hawk watch sign and look for the birds soaring in the sky. You may notice sounds of the roads on either side of this trail, but after a while you don't really hear them anymore (maybe because your heart is beating loudly in your chest!). Some sections are a looser shale, so watch your footing. Just before 2 miles, there is a split in which hikers go to the right and bikers to the left. On your right is the Arthur Lakes Lookout.

Arthur Lakes was a geologist, artist, and fossil hunter who lived in the area in the late 1800s. In March 1877, Lakes was planning to measure the rock layers of the Dakota Ridge when he and his friend, Henry C. Beckwith, discovered what they thought was a fossilized log. It turned out to be a dinosaur bone, marking the beginning of myriad dinosaur discoveries in the West. Lakes went on to find the first

Walking on the top of the hogback means widespread views of Red Rocks Park and beyond.

apatosaurus, stegosaurus (Colorado's state dinosaur), diplodocus, and a small crocodile, *Diplosaurus felix.*

Shortly after the lookout, head downhill and walk left down the paved road to see the dinosaur tracks. This is part of the Dinosaur Ridge Trail. The three-toed print you'll see was made by a type of hadrosaur (duck-billed dinosaur). They weighed about three tons and were 25 feet long. The tracks were made when the ground here was level and part of a tidal flat. Besides dinosaur tracks, the rock face has squiggles and bumps from the shrimp, worms, and other crawlers that burrowed into the wet sand and mud. Take your time to read the informative signs and learn more about the area before turning around and heading back.

Miles and Directions

0.0 From the south end of the parking lot, start at the Matthews/Winters Park Trailhead.

0.2 Make a sharp right at the gate.

0.6 Arrive at the hawk watch.

0.9 Come to an intersection with the Zorro Trail; continue straight.

1.9 Follow the sign and stay to the right.

2.0 Arrive at the Arthur Lakes Lookout.

2.1 Turn left onto the paved Dinosaur Ridge Trail.

2.3 Arrive at the first dinosaur tracks.

2.5 Turn around and return the way you came.

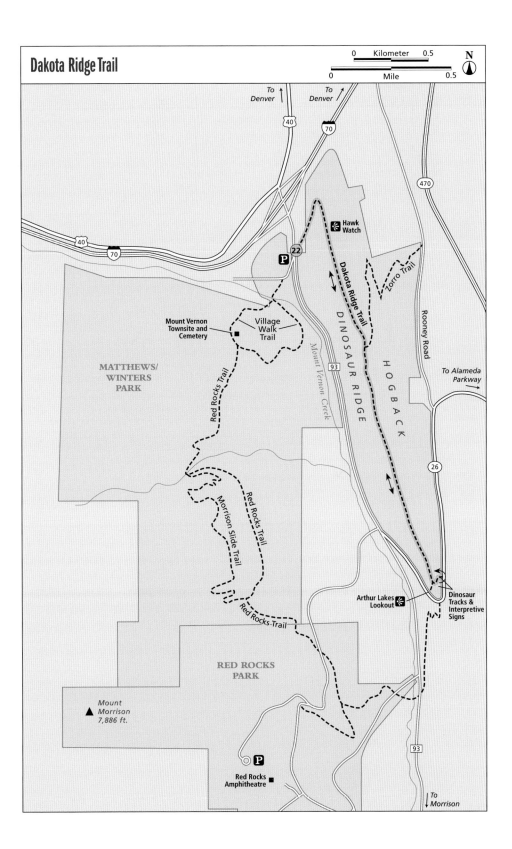

Dakota Ridge Trail

0   Kilometer   0.5

0   Mile   0.5

N

To Denver

To Denver

40

70

470

Hawk Watch

22

P

Dakota Ridge Trail

Zorro Trail

Rooney Road

Mount Vernon Townsite and Cemetery

Village Walk Trail

DINOSAUR RIDGE

H O G B A C K

MATTHEWS/ WINTERS PARK

Mount Vernon Creek

93

To Alameda Parkway

Red Rocks Trail

26

Morrison Slide Trail

Red Rocks Trail

Arthur Lakes Lookout

Dinosaur Tracks & Interpretive Signs

Red Rocks Trail

RED ROCKS PARK

Mount Morrison 7,886 ft.

P

93

Red Rocks Amphitheatre

To Morrison

This area is known as the best dinosaur track site in the entire country due to its quantity and quality.

4.0 Come to the intersection with the Zorro Trail; continue straight.

4.9 Arrive back at the trailhead.

Additional Route Options

You can add additional mileage here by going past the trail back up the hill after you see the dinosaur prints and continuing south on Dinosaur Ridge Road. When the road curves west, cross the road to pick up the Dakota Ridge Trail again on the south side for another 0.3 mile (one way). You'll have to turn around at the Dakota Ridge South Trail, as that's for mountain bikers only.

23 Mount Galbraith Loop via Cedar Gulch Trail

This trail is just outside of Golden and offers a lot of bang for your buck. It's not too difficult, but offers a decent amount of elevation gain as you walk through a lush riparian section, among meadows and wildflowers, and back via a cool forest. Wildlife such as deer, elk, a variety of birds, and even bighorn sheep have been spotted at the park. You'll also get a bird's-eye view of Golden and the Table Mountains.

Start: Mount Galbraith Park Trailhead
Distance: 4.2-mile lollipop
Difficulty: Moderate
Elevation gain: 928 feet
Hiking time: 1.5–2.5 hours
Trail surface: Mostly dirt, some rocky spots
Seasons/schedule: Year-round. The park is open 1 hour before sunrise to 1 hour after sunset.
Fees and permits: None
Other trail users: None
Canine compatibility: Dogs must be on leash at all times.

Land status: Jefferson County Open Space
Trail contact: Jeffco Open Space; (303) 271-5925; www.jeffco.us/1335/Mount-Galbraith-Park
Maps: Mount Galbraith Park map
Nearest town: Golden
Cell service: Good in parking lot; spotty on trail
Special considerations: If the main parking lot is full, you can park in some areas on the south side of Golden Gate Canyon Road—just be sure to heed any No Parking signs.

Finding the trailhead: From the intersection of US 6 and I-25 in Denver, drive west on US 6 for 8.8 miles. Keep left to continue on US 6 as it converges with US 40 for 0.8 mile. Continue straight on US 6 for 3.2 miles. After crossing CO 58, US 6 will turn into CO 93 north. Continue straight for 1.4 miles. Turn left on Golden Gate Canyon Road for 1.3 miles and the Mount Galbraith Park parking lot will be on your left. GPS: N39 46.43' / W105 15.25'

The Hike

Start on the Cedar Gulch Trail in the parking lot. The trail winds along the cottonwood-lined creek and then switchbacks up for a steep uphill climb right away. Curving around the mountain's east side, there is a bit of rock scrambling involved, but just keep following the trail around. At 1.3 miles, stay straight to walk the Mount Galbraith Loop clockwise. After you go around the corner, stay straight and high—the path left and down is a neighborhood access trail.

> **Mount Galbraith was named after Den S. Galbraith (1918–1977), a historian, author, and professor at the Colorado School of Mines.**

Mount Galbraith is the tallest "peak" near Golden, offering views of the town to the east, as shown here, and Mount Blue Sky (formerly Mount Evans) to the west.

One of the best viewpoints is at 1.6 miles. Walk down the spur trail on your left to the tree and a small rocky outcropping. Straight ahead is the city of Golden and the Table Mountains. To the west, you'll often see paragliders. Head back to the Mount Galbraith Loop and stay on the lower, left trail.

While the east side of the loop is mostly wildflower meadows with some trees sprinkled in, the west side is mostly forested and rocky. Continue down and just after a rock pile at 2.3 miles, the trail veers left and down (there's an arrow on the tree in front of you). A little farther, you'll start to notice that many of the trees to your left are what remains from a forest fire that raged through the area in March 2011. Strong winds and dry vegetation spread the fire quickly, destroying more than 1,000 acres between Clear Creek and Golden Gate Canyons and forcing the evacuation of several neighborhoods.

Continue through the forest until the loop meets back up with the Cedar Gulch Trail.

Turn left and walk back the way you came.

Downed trees from the 2011 fire on the west side of the Mount Galbraith Loop.

Mount Galbraith Loop via Cedar Gulch Trail

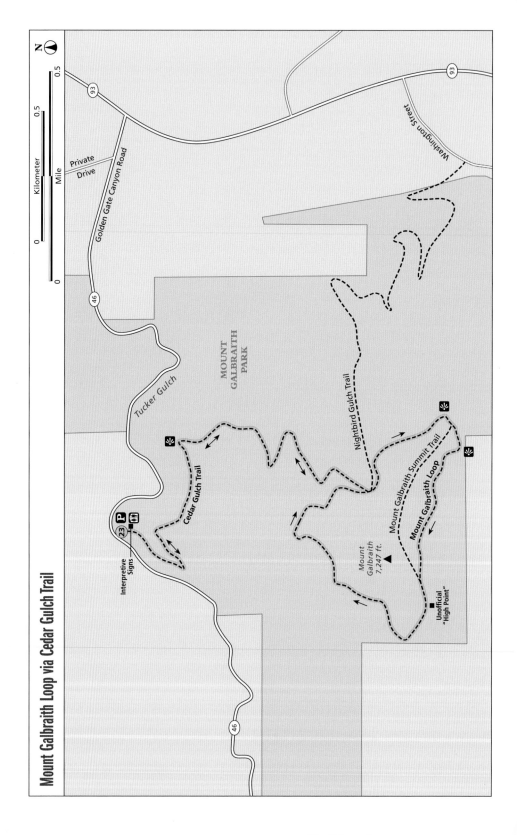

Wildflowers, like the reddish-orange wholeleaf Indian paintbrush, are abundant on the meadow sections of the trail.

Miles and Directions

0.0 Start at the Mount Galbraith Park Trailhead.

1.3 Come to an intersection with the Mount Galbraith Loop and social trail; stay straight to continue on the higher trail.

1.6 Arrive at a viewpoint. Backtrack to the main trail and stay to the left on the lower trail.

1.8 The Mount Galbraith Summit Trail goes up to the right. Stay straight.

2.2 Stay straight to continue on the Mount Galbraith Loop.

2.3 Follow the trail around to the right, then look for an arrow on a tree to turn left.

2.8 Follow the trail to the right.

3.0 Come to the intersection with the Cedar Gulch Trail; turn left to return to parking lot.

4.2 Arrive back at the trailhead.

Additional Route Options

While this trail encircles the mountain, you can summit Mount Galbraith. It adds on slightly over 0.1 mile. At 1.8 miles, turn right up Mount Galbraith Summit Trail, then left for 0.3 mile until you reach the summit at 7,247 feet. Continue on that trail and it will rejoin the Mount Galbraith Loop in just under 0.2 mile.

24 Peaks to Plains Trail–Gateway Trailhead

The vision is that the Peaks to Plains (P2P) Trail will stretch for 65 miles from the summit of Loveland Pass at 12,000 feet to the South Platte Trail in Denver. Currently, there are two completed sections with a third estimated to be completed by 2025. The section I chose is a shorter distance but offers an interesting history.

Start: Gateway Trailhead, Clear Creek Canyon Park

Distance: 2.7-mile loop

Difficulty: Easy

Elevation gain: 249 feet

Hiking time: 1 hour or less

Trail surface: Paved and dirt; some wooden planks on Welch Ditch Trail

Seasons/schedule: Year-round. The park is open 1 hour before sunrise to 1 hour after sunset.

Fees and permits: None

Other trail users: Mountain bikers

Canine compatibility: Dogs must be on leash at all times.

Land status: Jefferson County Open Space

Trail contact: Jeffco Open Space; (303) 271-5925; www.jeffco.us/3792/Peaks-to-Plains-Trail

Maps: Clear Creek Canyon Park map

Nearest town: Golden

Cell service: Good

Special considerations: If the parking lot is full at the Gateway Trailhead, continue on Clear Creek Canyon Road for 0.7 mile to the Tunnel 1 Trailhead and walk the route in reverse. There are steps to access the trail on the west side of the parking lot but an ADA-accessible ramp on the east side. Only certain sections of the creek are open for tubing—always pay attention to the signage if you plan to get into the water.

Finding the trailhead: From the intersection of US 6 and I-25 in Denver, drive west on US 6 for 8.8 miles. Keep left to continue on US 6 as it converges with US 40 for 0.8 mile. Continue straight on US 6 for 3.2 miles. Turn left at the light to stay on US 6/Clear Creek Canyon Road. After 0.2 mile, turn into the parking lot on your left. GPS: N39 45.98' / W105 10.42'

The Hike

The trail starts at the southwest section of the parking lot. Go down the metal steps and continue straight. You'll soon cross a bridge and if the weather is warm enough, you may see some tubers putting in around here. Turn right after the bridge to follow the creek. There are several spur trails to the right that lead down to the water.

At 0.7 mile, cross the Tough Cuss Bridge and see the second parking lot just before Tunnel 1. Shortly after, another bridge will be on your left. Continue straight past this bridge for now. Again, there are several great spots to head down and sit on a rock for a while to listen to the rushing water. When you see construction and the trail is closed, turn around. This is the next section of the

> **The Peaks to Plains project is the largest capital project in Jeffco Open Space's fifty-year history.**

The Peaks to Plains Trail runs along Clear Creek, which is a popular tubing spot in Golden.

P2P, called Huntsman Gulch. When it opens in 2025, this segment will connect Tunnel 1 to Huntsman Gulch via almost 3 miles of new trail.

You'll come back to the bridge to cross Clear Creek at 1.4 miles. Take the steps up and turn left onto the Welch Ditch Trail. Welch Ditch was hand-constructed by Charles C. Welch in 1885 and was able to divert 26 cubic feet of water per second through the flume that is now the trail. It was a major source of water for brewing beer, growing crops, assisting mining, and servicing both livestock and the communities near Denver. The posts that you see were originally made from local lumber but were replaced by Douglas fir and treated with creosote to waterproof and preserve them.

Follow the old flume-turned-trail high above Clear Creek until you arrive at a sign that denotes climbing access straight ahead (Clear Creek Canyon is a popular climbing area). Turn left and go down the wooden steps. They are well made but can be uneven, so some may want to use the railing. Turn right to go slightly downhill and back the way you came.

Peak to Plains Trail—Gateway Trailhead

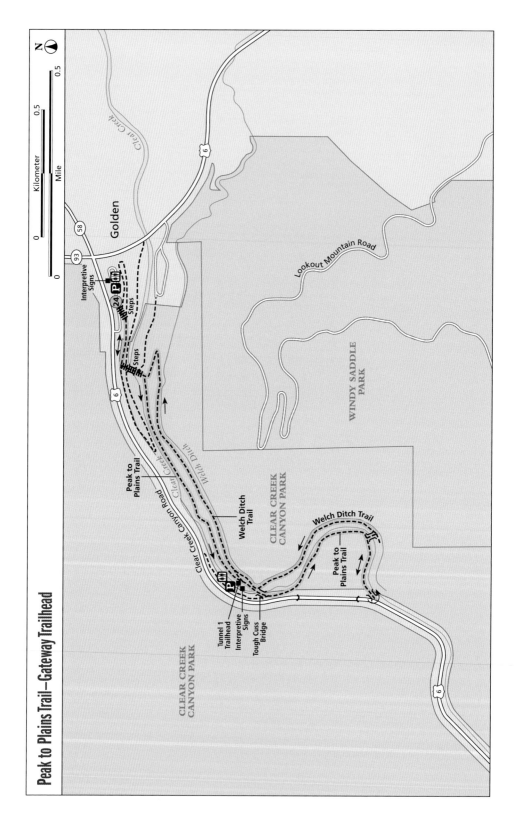

The Welch Ditch Trail follows an old flume from the 1800s.

Miles and Directions

0.0 Start at the Gateway Trailhead.

0.1 Turn left and go over the bridge, then turn right after crossing the bridge.

0.7 Stay straight and go over the Tough Cuss Bridge.

1.3 Turn around at the Huntsman Gulch Bridge.

1.4 Turn right to cross the bridge and then turn left onto the Welch Ditch Trail.

1.9 Go through the gate; shortly after turn left, go down the steps, and turn right onto a paved walkway.

2.5 Turn left to cross the bridge and then turn right after the bridge.

2.7 Turn left to go up steps and arrive back at the trailhead.

Additional Route Options

If you're looking for a longer walk or want to add on more miles, drive 9 more miles west on US 6/Clear Creek Canyon Road to the Big Easy Trailhead. This section of the P2P is 7 miles out and back.

25 Belcher Hill and Mustang Trails

The largest park in the Jefferson County Open Space system, White Ranch Park near Golden is a popular spot for hikers, runners, and mountain bikers to get outside. There are 20-plus miles of trails for a variety of levels, and the Belcher Hill and Mustang Trails go through a wetlands area (depending on the season), past a private ranch, and up Belcher Hill for views of Denver and the foothills.

Start: White Ranch Park East Trailhead
Distance: 8.8-mile lollipop
Difficulty: Moderate
Elevation gain: 1,948 feet
Hiking time: 2.5-4 hours
Trail surface: Dirt with some rocky sections
Seasons/schedule: Year-round. The park is open 1 hour before sunrise to 1 hour after sunset.
Fees and permits: None
Other trail users: Equestrians and mountain bikers

Canine compatibility: Dogs must be on leash at all times.
Land status: Jefferson County Open Space
Trail contact: Jeffco Open Space; (303) 271-5925; www.jeffco.us/1437/White-Ranch-Park
Maps: White Ranch Park map
Nearest town: Golden
Cell service: Spotty
Special considerations: Trails may be closed due to weather or muddy conditions. It's important to follow the leash rules here because there may be free-range cattle on the trail.

Finding the trailhead: From the intersection of I-25 and I-70 in Denver, drive west on I-70 for 8.4 miles. Take exit 265 for CO 58 toward Golden/Central City. Continue onto CO 58 for 4.7 miles, then turn right onto CO 93 for 1.8 miles. Turn left onto Pine Ridge Road for 1.8 miles and continue straight into the parking lot. GPS: N39 47.93' / W105 14.90'

The Hike

Starting at the trailhead, walk through the gate and tallgrass meadow on the Belcher Hill Trail. Cross a private road and then pass through another gate (be sure to close gates behind you). This wetland area crosses Van Bibber Creek and is thick with plants, shrubs, and trees. It's a narrow, sandy trail, so just keep your eyes up and be aware of any mountain bikers that might be coming through. This section also runs along a private ranch with free-range cattle (hence the gates). I've seen cows in the bushes and on the hills to the left, so also be aware that there could be large animals roaming about. Keep pets and young children close on this part of the trail.

> Van Bibber Creek was named after Isaac Van Bibber, who had a farm along the water. There's a park of the same name in the town of Arvada and a trail that follows the creek about 5 miles through several neighborhoods.

The trail starts though the gate.

After about 0.5 mile, the trail gets closer to the hillside and heads toward the canyon. At a mile in, you'll start climbing up Belcher Hill. Follow the trail left when the Whippletree Trail comes in from your right and keep going up. The grade here isn't terribly steep—you'll just continue climbing on the main trail until almost 4 miles.

At 2.4 miles, continue straight on Belcher Hill to the junction with the Mustang Trail. Stay straight to take this loop counterclockwise. This next section, on the ridge of Belcher Hill, features views of Denver to the east and the foothills to the west. Follow this part of the trail until it meets the Sawmill Trail and go straight through the intersection to stay on Belcher Hill. In 0.8 mile, the trail will T. Go left on the Mustang Trail. You'll pass the Sawmill Trail again, but keep going straight to finish the loop. Once you get back to the Belcher Hill Trail, turn right and return the way you came.

Belcher Hill and Mustang Trails

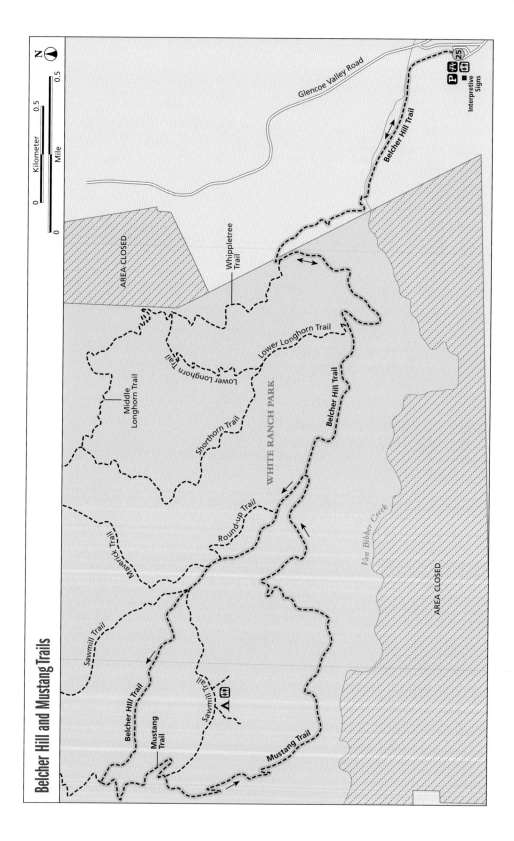

Glencoe Valley Road

Belcher Hill Trail

Interpretive Signs

P 🚻 🚻 25

AREA CLOSED

Whippletree Trail

Middle Longhorn Trail

Lower Longhorn Trail

Lower Longhorn Trail

Shorthorn Trail

WHITE RANCH PARK

Belcher Hill Trail

Van Bibber Creek

Round-up Trail

Maverick Trail

AREA CLOSED

Sawmill Trail

Belcher Hill Trail

Mustang Trail

Sawmill Trail

🚻 ⛺

Mustang Trail

N

Kilometer
0   0.5

0   0.5
Mile

Watch for free-range cows on the first section of the Belcher Hill Trail.

Miles and Directions

0.0 Start at the East Trailhead and go through the gate, being sure to close it after you pass through.

0.1 Cross a private road and go through another gate, closing it as well.

1.1 Follow the trail around to the left and straight past the intersection with the Whipple-tree Trail.

1.8 Continue straight past the Lower Longhorn Trail.

2.4 Come to a junction with the Mustang Trail; continue straight.

2.9 Continue straight past the Maverick Trail.

3.0 Come to an intersection with the Sawmill Trail going right and left; continue straight.

3.8 The trail Ts with the Mustang Trail; go left.

4.4 Continue straight past the Sawmill Trail.

6.4 Rejoin the Belcher Hill Trail; turn right to return to the trailhead.

8.8 Arrive back at the trailhead.

Like many trails in the Front Range, you'll see interesting layered rock formations while hiking at White Ranch Park.

Additional Route Options

If want to cut out 0.5 mile and/or you need to make a pit stop mid-hike, turn left on the Sawmill Trail at mile 3.0 and stop at the campground. Continue west and then take a left on the Mustang Trail to finish the loop and head back. You can also easily extend this hike by taking any of the options that intersect. Pick up a map at the trailhead or look online and plan your route before setting out.

26 Evergreen Mountain Trail

Alderfer/Three Sisters Park is a popular spot for hikers and boulderers. The former homestead became a big project in land preservation over the years, and today has more trails per acre than any of the parks in the foothills. The Evergreen Mountain Trail takes you through ponderosa and lodgepole pine forest to some seriously stunning vistas at the top.

Start: West Trailhead, Alderfer/Three Sisters Park
Distance: 4.6 miles out and back with small loop at the end
Difficulty: Moderate
Elevation gain: 810 feet
Hiking time: 1.5–2.5 hours
Trail surface: Dirt
Seasons/schedule: Year-round. The park is open 1 hour before sunrise to 1 hour after sunset.
Fees and permits: None

Other trail users: Mountain bikers
Canine compatibility: Dogs must be on leash at all times.
Land status: Jefferson County Open Space
Trail contact: Jeffco Open Space; (303) 271-5925; www.jeffco.us/980/ Alderfer-Three-Sisters-Park
Maps: Alderfer/Three Sisters Park map
Nearest town: Evergreen
Cell service: Good at trailhead; spotty on trail
Special considerations: None

Finding the trailhead: From the intersection of US 6 and I-25 in Denver, drive west on US 6 for 8.8 miles. Exit onto I-70 toward Grand Junction for 9.3 miles. Use the right two lanes to take exit 252 for CO 74 toward Evergreen Parkway. Continue on CO 74 for 7.4 miles, then turn right onto CR 73 for 0.5 mile. Take a slight right onto South Buffalo Park Road for 2.2 miles. Turn right onto South Le Masters Road and into the parking lot. GPS: N39 37.37' / W105 21.60'

The Hike

Several trails start from this parking lot; the trail for this hike starts on the south side of Buffalo Park Road. There's a path near the restrooms that leads to the road; cross it and turn right onto the Wild Iris Loop. Walk on the narrow trail through the meadow and when you come to a junction, turn right and then right again onto the Evergreen Mountain West Trail. Wildflowers dot the trail in the forest, and if you're lucky, you might even spot a Colorado blue columbine, like the lone flower I found on my recent hike here.

> The Colorado blue columbine is the state flower and one of my favorites because I don't see it that often. This perennial plant loves moist areas, whether that's a meadow or forest, and blooms from April until July. They are most commonly found at elevations between 7,000 and 12,000 feet, but I usually only see them at the higher end of the spectrum.

The view from the Summit Trail near the peak of Evergreen Mountain.

At 1 mile, the trail gets steeper and rockier, and then you'll take a right and stay higher.

The other trail leads to the East Trailhead. Right around 2 miles, there will be a short scenic-view spur to your right, and then you'll start the Summit Trail loop after that. Go counterclockwise (the path on the right) and take in the views along the way. There are several points where you can scramble onto the rocks for a better look. The high point is 8,555 feet on the southwest side of the loop at 2.4 miles. Follow the trail around, then turn right once you complete the loop and head down the mountain to return as you came.

Miles and Directions

0.0   Start at the West Trailhead on south side of Buffalo Park Road.

0.3   Bear right and then right again onto the Evergreen Mountain Trail West.

1.3   Stay on the higher Summit Trail to the right.

1.9   Arrive at a scenic spur trail.

2.1   Take the path to the right.

2.4   Arrive at the high point of Evergreen Mountain.

2.6   Turn right.

Much of the trail winds through the lodgepole pine forest. JACOB PREBLE

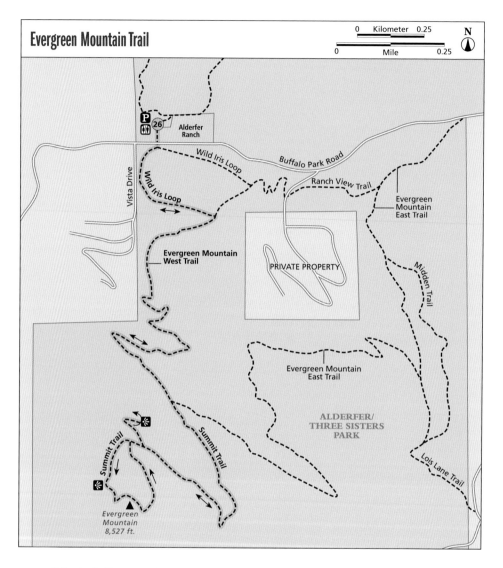

3.2 At the Evergreen Mountain East Trail, stay straight.

4.2 Stay left to get back on the Wild Iris Loop. Follow around and cross Buffalo Park Road.

4.6 Arrive back at the trailhead.

Additional Route Options

For a large loop instead of an out-and-back, take the Evergreen Mountain East Trail on your way back from the Summit Trail at 3.2 miles for 2.3 miles. Turn left on the Ranch View Trail and follow it 0.4 mile back to the Wild Iris Loop to finish where you started.

27 Sunny Aspen Trail and Lodge Pole Loop

For a shorter hike close to town that will get your heart pumping, head out to Meyer Ranch Park. Located just off US 285, this trail is easy to access and get in a quick hike year-round. It's also a great spot for trail runners looking to get in a couple laps after work during the longer summer days.

Start: Meyer Ranch Park Trailhead
Distance: 2.4-mile loop
Difficulty: Moderate
Elevation gain: 436 feet
Hiking time: 0.75–1 hour
Trail surface: Dirt
Seasons/schedule: Year-round. The park is open 1 hour before sunrise to 1 hour after sunset.
Fees and permits: None
Other trail users: Mountain bikers

Canine compatibility: Dogs must be on leash at all times.
Land status: Jefferson County Open Space
Trail contact: Jeffco Open Space; (303) 271-5925; www.jeffco.us/1304/Meyer-Ranch-Park
Maps: Meyer Ranch Park map
Nearest town: Aspen Park
Cell service: Good
Special considerations: There are no restrooms at the parking lot, but there is a restroom building 0.1 mile up the trail.

Finding the trailhead: From the intersection of US 6 and I-25 in Denver, drive west on US 6 for 8.8 miles. Exit onto I-70 toward Grand Junction for 1 mile. Use the right two lanes to take exit 260 for CO 470 toward Colorado Springs. Merge onto CO 470 east for 5.1 miles. Take exit 5A onto US 285 south toward Fairplay and continue for 11.4 miles. Take the South Turkey Creek Road exit and turn left. The parking lot will be on your right. GPS: N39 32.77' / W105 16.32'

The Hike

Meyer Ranch has a couple different loops through the park—this one winds through the forest and has a nice picnic shelter. Starting at the trailhead, walk up Owl's Perch and past the restrooms. Continue uphill and go straight onto the Lodge Pole Loop. This deceptively uphill trail levels out after just over 0.5 mile of climbing.

Come to the picnic shelter at 1 mile, where the Old Ski Run Trail comes in from the left. For two years, from 1940 until 1942, Meyer Ranch was part of the Mount Lugo Ski Area. The remains of the old rope-tow motor can be seen on the Old Ski Run Trail. Surrounded by aspens, this junction is a lovely place in the fall when the leaves are changing.

Just over a mile, take a sharp left to rejoin the Lodge Pole Loop. At 1.4 miles, take a sharp right at the junction with the neighborhood access trail. Stay straight across the logging road and bear left at 1.8 miles. You have two options for your return route via Owl's Perch: go straight and back to the restrooms or turn left, which also joins right before the restrooms. The left path takes a wider route and has a bench that

This is one of the many Front Range hikes that are accessible year-round (and is a popular sledding area in the winter when the snow piles up on the north-facing hill).

looks out toward the north. When the trails meet back up again, go left and downhill to the parking lot.

Miles and Directions

0.0 Start at the Meyer Ranch Park Trailhead.

0.2 Turn right just after the restrooms.

0.4 Go straight onto the loop.

0.5 Turn left onto the Sunny Aspen Trail.

1.0 Arrive at the picnic shelter and junction with the Old Ski Run Trail; go straight.

1.3 Make a sharp left back onto the Lodge Pole Loop.

1.4 Make a sharp right at the neighborhood access trail.

1.6 Stay straight on the access road.

1.8 Bear left.

2.0 Turn left onto Owl's Perch.

2.1 Rejoin the Lodge Pole Loop.

2.2 Turn left to return to the parking lot.

2.4 Arrive back at the trailhead.

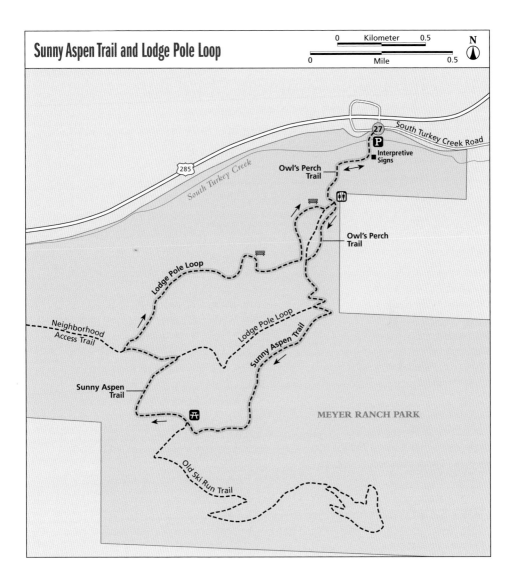

Sunny Aspen Trail and Lodge Pole Loop

South Turkey Creek Road

Interpretive Signs

Owl's Perch Trail

Owl's Perch Trail

285

South Turkey Creek

Lodge Pole Loop

Neighborhood Access Trail

Lodge Pole Loop

Sunny Aspen Trail

Sunny Aspen Trail

MEYER RANCH PARK

Old Ski Run Trail

Additional Route Options

At 1 mile, take a left onto the Old Ski Run Trail. It's 0.7 mile one way and then there's a 0.5-mile loop at the end. Near the top you can see 14,268-foot Mount Blue Sky (formerly Mount Evans) to the west.

28 Staunton Ranch, Old Mill, and Border Line Trails—Staunton State Park

One of the newer state parks in Colorado (it opened in 2013), Staunton State Park is one of the most underrated hiking spots in the Front Range. The park has nearly 30 miles of trails across 1,720 acres, and habitats range from grassy meadows and peaceful streams to mixed conifer forests and granite cliffs reaching over 9,579 feet. This hike includes an old mill site (and a couple historic cabins if you want to take a side trail), one of the highest points in the park, and gives you a feel for the diversity that this park has to offer.

Start: Staunton Ranch Trailhead
Distance: 7.8-mile lollipop
Difficulty: Moderate
Elevation gain: 1,230 feet
Hiking time: 2.5–4 hours
Trail surface: Dirt and some rocky sections
Seasons/schedule: Year-round; best in summer and fall. Day-use hours are 6 a.m. to 10 p.m.
Fees and permits: Daily entrance fee or annual state parks pass required
Other trail users: None on Old Mill Trail; mountain bikers on the hike's other trails

Canine compatibility: Dogs must be on leash at all times.
Land status: Staunton State Park
Trail contact: Staunton State Park; (303) 816-0912; https://cpw.state.co.us/placestogo/parks/Staunton
Maps: Staunton State Park map
Nearest town: Pine Junction
Cell service: Spotty in parking lot; none on trail
Special considerations: There are ChargePoint electric vehicle chargers in the visitor center parking lot. The park also has a Track-Chair program to make the trails more accessible to all.

Finding the trailhead: From the intersection of US 6 and I-25 in Denver, drive west on US 6 for 8.8 miles. Exit onto I-70 toward Grand Junction for 1 mile. Use the right two lanes to take exit 260 for CO 470 toward Colorado Springs. Merge onto CO 470 for 5.1 miles, then take exit 5A onto US 285 toward Fairplay and continue for 18.5 miles. Take the exit toward Elk Creek Road, then turn right onto Elk Creek Road and continue for 1.3 miles. Turn right into Staunton State Park. Stay on the main road for 0.5 mile and then turn right into the Upper Parking Lot. GPS: N39 30.01' / W105 22.70'

The Hike

There are many reasons why Staunton State Park is a great place to hike, but two of the biggest reasons for me are the diversity of the land and the historic value. The Ute and Cheyenne once lived in the area, and you can still spot their spirit trees, marking water, resources, and trade routes. The heart of the park is Staunton Ranch, where you can see historic cabins dating back to the homestead and mining days. Frances H.

The beginning and the end of the trail meanders through open meadows.

Staunton lived on the land with her parents and donated it just before her death in 1989 because she wanted the area to "be preserved, in perpetuity, for public benefit, as a natural wilderness-type park . . . typifying Colorado's most beautiful mountain forest and meadow region."

    The Staunton Ranch Trail takes you through a mix of meadow and forest, prime spots to see deer, elk, and turkeys. Follow the path across the service road and past two spurs down to historic cabins—or make the stop if you'd like to see them. You'll also pass several climbing areas with more than 400 routes in total, including sport, trad, bouldering, and even ice climbing.

    At 1.8 miles, you'll come to a trail junction and can take either direction for the loop portion of the hike. I took a right to climb the wide, rocky Old Mill Trail in the beginning. The creek follows along to your right and you'll eventually walk straight up to the fence around the old mill site. At the top of the old mill site, take a left past the bunkhouse and

> Archibald Staunton, Frances Staunton's father, purchased the mill in the 1930s. The workers here helped operate a large cable system that transported logs across the valley.

The view overlooking the ranch and out to the mountains is worth the 0.1-mile walk on the spur trail, even on a rainy day. JACOB PREBLE

onto the Border Line Trail. There's also some old equipment strewn about and a single chair sitting in an opening to the south.

There are a few stream crossings in this section as you head toward the high point. At 3.6 miles, there is a T in the trail. Go left for 0.1 mile to the Staunton Ranch Overlook, one of the highest points in the park at 9,410 feet. Once you take in the views, trace your steps back on the spur trail and go straight through the T to continue on the loop. Follow the trail to the left when you encounter the Rusty Buckle Trail. (#769), then left again to go back down Staunton Ranch. Follow the trail past the Staunton Rocks climbing area, past the intersection with the Old Mill Trail, and all the way back to the trailhead.

Miles and Directions

0.0 Start at the Staunton Ranch Trailhead.

0.5 Pass the trash can and go straight through an intersection with a service road.

1.0 Stay straight on the Staunton Ranch Trail.

1.5 Stay straight on the Staunton Ranch Trail.

Six workers lived in the bunkhouse at the old mill site.

Staunton Ranch, Old Mill, and Borderline Trails—Staunton State Park

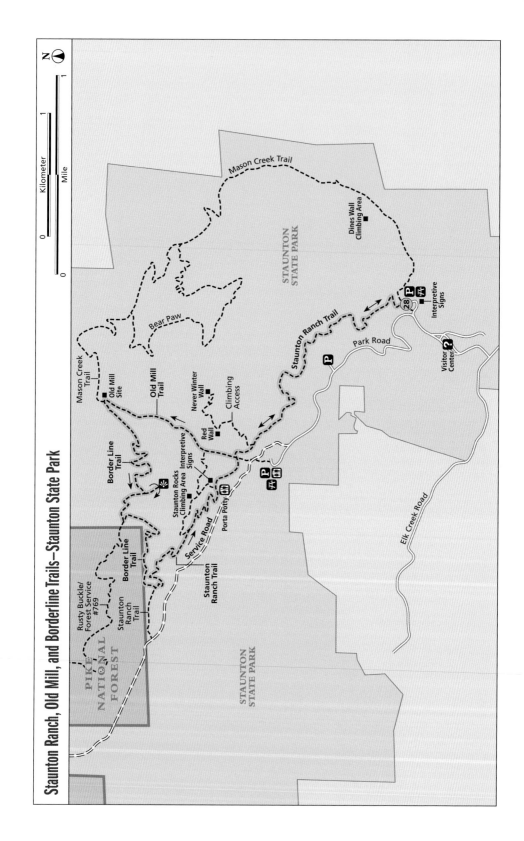

1.7 Stay straight to pass the climbing access trails.

1.8 Turn right onto the Old Mill Trail.

2.0 Stay straight to pass the climbing access trail.

2.5 Arrive at the old mill site.

2.6 Come to a junction with the Border Line Trail; turn left.

3.6 The trail Ts; go left to the Staunton Ranch Overlook. Return via the spur trail and go straight through the T.

4.0 Come to a junction with the Rusty Buckle Trail (#769); follow the trail to the left.

4.8 Turn left to rejoin the Staunton Ranch Trail.

5.2 Go left.

6.0 Go straight through the intersection with the Old Mill Trail and follow Staunton Ranch back to the trailhead. Continue straight past the climbing access spurs.

7.3 Follow the trail to the right and go straight across the service road.

7.8 Arrive back at the trailhead.

Additional Route Options

There are many options if you want to either shorten or lengthen this route. I'd suggest checking out the park map online if you want some ideas ahead of time. One addition I would recommend, though, is taking the spur trail at 1 mile to see the historic cabin. The trail adds 0.7 mile each way, but gives you a glimpse of the homestead life of the 1800s.

29 St. Mary's Glacier and James Peak

If you are considering hiking one of Colorado's 14ers (peaks over 14,000 feet), summiting a 13,000-plus-foot peak is a good training run. As an added bonus, this hike goes past St. Mary's Glacier, which unfortunately won't be around for too much longer, so see it now while you can.

Start: St. Mary's Glacier Trailhead
Distance: 7.3 miles out and back
Difficulty: Strenuous
Elevation gain: 2,880 feet
Hiking time: 5-7 hours
Trail surface: Dirt and some rocky sections in the beginning and as you get closer to the peak
Seasons/schedule: Summer to early fall
Fees and permits: Fee to park at St. Mary's Glacier Trailhead
Other trail users: None

Canine compatibility: Dogs must be on leash at all times.
Land status: James Peak Wilderness
Trail contact: Clear Creek Ranger District; (303) 567-4382; www.fs.usda.gov/recarea/arp/recarea/?recid=28372
Maps: National Geographic Trails Illustrated #103: Winter Park/Central City/Rollins Pass
Nearest town: Empire
Cell service: None
Special considerations: Park in pay lots only; do not park on the road.

Finding the trailhead: From the intersection of US 6 and I-25 in Denver, drive west on US 6 for 8.8 miles. Exit onto I-70 toward Grand Junction for 23.3 miles. Take exit 238 for Fall River Road. Turn right on Fall River Road for 8.6 miles. The parking area will be on the left side of the road. GPS: N39 49.68' / W105 38.54'

The Hike

It's only about a mile from the trailhead to St. Mary's Lake, fed by the glacier of the same name. This part of the hike is accessible almost year-round, and many skiers and snowboarders trek up here in the spring to catch a few more rides before the season ends. Despite what the name suggests, the "glacier" is actually a semipermanent snowfield because it isn't moving. Unfortunately, it *is* disappearing, and the entire snowfield may melt away in the next twenty-five to fifty years.

Continuing past the glacier at almost 11,000 feet, you're above treeline for the rest of the trail, so if there is any questionable weather in the forecast, either get out there

James Peak was named after Edwin James, a physician and botanist who was the first to describe many of the plants in the Rocky Mountains. He traveled to Colorado as part of the 1819 US Army Expedition. The James Peak area became part of the National Wilderness Preservation System in 2002.

Be sure to stop and look back over the glacier and lake when you get to the top.

early or save this one for another day. Stay straight across the tundra and head toward the four-wheel-drive Kingston Peak Road.

Follow the James Peak South Trail. At the base of the mountain, look for a cairn-marked trail slightly south. This is the easiest way up. The more direct route is littered with boulders and involves more scrambling without a defined trail. At the saddle, turn north and push to the peak. The trail is less defined here, but the route is obvious.

After you've caught your breath and soaked up the views, return the way you came.

St. Mary's Glacier and James Peak

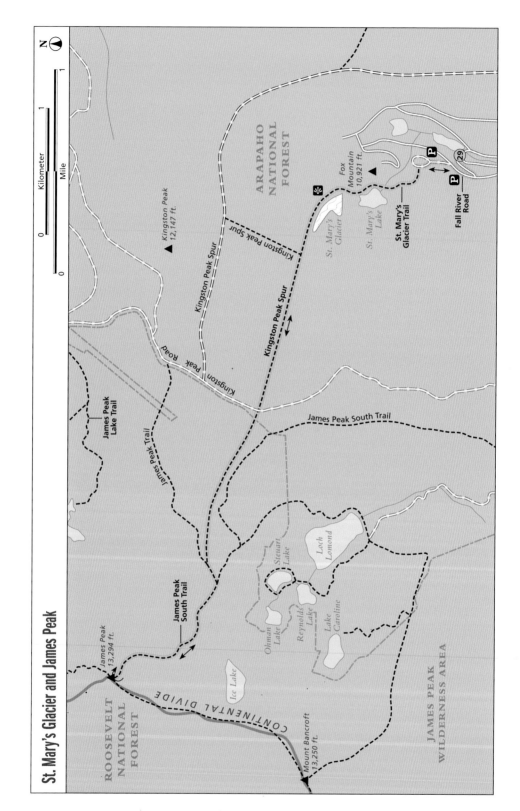

N

Kilometer
Mile

Kingston Peak
12,147 ft.

Kingston Peak Spur

Kingston Peak Spur

Kingston Peak Spur

Kingston Peak Road

James Peak Lake Trail

James Peak Trail

James Peak South Trail

James Peak South Trail

ARAPAHO NATIONAL FOREST

St. Mary's Glacier

St. Mary's Lake

Fox Mountain
10,921 ft.

St. Mary's Glacier Trail

Fall River Road

P

P

29

Stewart Lake

Ohman Lake

Reynolds Lake

Lake Caroline

Loch Lomond

Ice Lake

James Peak
13,294 ft.

CONTINENTAL DIVIDE

Mount Bancroft
13,250 ft.

ROOSEVELT NATIONAL FOREST

JAMES PEAK WILDERNESS AREA

St. Mary's Lake is very pretty in the late spring when the snow and ice start to melt.

Miles and Directions

0.0 Start at the St. Mary's Glacier Trailhead.

0.2 Turn left at the top of the hill.

0.4 Bear left.

0.8 Arrive at St. Mary's Glacier. Continue up and around the right side.

1.3 Come to a junction with the Kingston Peak Spur; continue straight.

2.0 Cross the four-wheel-drive road.

2.2 Look for a cairn-marked trail slightly south.

2.9 Turn north and head for the peak.

3.8 Arrive at the top of James Peak. Return the way you came.

7.3 Arrive back at the trailhead.

Additional Route Options

If weather starts to roll in or you change your mind about going all the way to the summit, the hike up to St. Mary's Glacier is a moderate and rocky 1.6 miles out and back.

30 Grays and Torreys Peaks

Grays and Torreys Peaks are popular first-timer 14ers for several reasons: you can easily bag two peaks in one day, they're close to Denver so you don't have to camp out or start driving the night before, and it's single-digit mileage. That being said, never take a 14,000-foot peak for granted. Train for it, bring plenty of water and extra layers, be prepared to bail if you start feeling altitude sickness, and plan to get off the summit by noon during the summer months. Summer is the highest risk for dangerous storms that can roll in quickly.

Start: Grays Peak Trailhead
Distance: 8.1 miles out and back
Difficulty: Strenuous
Elevation gain: 3,600 feet
Hiking time: 4–7 hours
Trail surface: Dirt, then rocky as you get closer to the top
Seasons/schedule: Summer to early fall
Fees and permits: None
Other trail users: None
Canine compatibility: Dogs must be on leash at all times. Do not bring your dog on a 14er if they are not in good hiking condition.
Land status: James Peak Wilderness
Trail contact: Clear Creek Ranger District; (303) 567-4382; www.fs.usda.gov/recarea/arp/recarea/?recid=28372

Maps: National Geographic Trails Illustrated #104: Idaho Springs/Loveland Pass
Nearest town: Georgetown
Cell service: None
Special considerations: There is no parking on the road leading to the trailhead. Pay attention to the signs or you will get ticketed. The only other parking is at the winter lot at the beginning of Stevens Gulch Road, requiring you to walk the extra 3 miles up to the trailhead. When you're above the treeline, the risk for a storm isn't just that you'll get rained on—it's downright dangerous to be around lightning at that elevation. Always pay attention to the weather forecast/radar and have a plan for getting off the mountain as quickly and safely as possible.

Finding the trailhead: From the intersection of US 6 and I-25 in Denver, drive west on US 6 for 8.8 miles. Exit onto I-70 toward Grand Junction for 39.5 miles, then take exit 221 toward Bakerville. Turn left onto East Bakerville Road and before Stevens Gulch Road you'll see the winter trailhead parking lot. If you have a low-clearance vehicle, you will need to park here and walk the 3 miles to the summer trailhead. Otherwise, continue on Stevens Gulch Road until you get to the trailhead's main parking area. GPS: N39 39.40' / W105 47.05'

The Hike

We assume that Indigenous people traveled these trails long before we did, and then miners after that, especially considering the remnants of the old Stevens mine can be seen at the base of nearby McClellan Mountain. But the first recorded ascent, and therefore the naming rights, goes to Charles Parry in 1861. He named the mountains after his friends Asa Gray and John Torrey. Not knowing this, a group of prospectors

Being on top of a 14er feels like you're on top of the world.

named Richard Irwin, John Baker, and William Fletcher Kelso tried to name Grays after Baker and Torreys after Irwin, but the original names prevailed. (Kelso chose a different, nearby peak to name after himself, and lucky for him, his name stuck.)

From the trailhead, cross Stevens Gulch Road and go over a bridge to get on the Grays Peak Trail (#54). The trail follows along Kelso Mountain, with views of your ultimate destination most of the way. At 1.5 miles, there's an informative sign that is the perfect place to take a break before you really get into the climbing. Go straight at the Kelso Ridge Trail intersection.

At 2.7 miles, turn left to stay on the Grays Peak Trail. You'll summit Grays Peak first—it's the one on the left. The bottom section of the trail is often wet, and when you start climbing the rocky switchbacks, you'll feel the gain in altitude quickly. After 3,000 feet of elevation gain in just 3.5 miles, you'll find yourself at the top of Grays. Enjoy the work you put in and take in the views—you've earned it!

Grays was my first 14er. I thought I was in decent shape, but it was still a challenge. I remember initially telling my hiking partner that I was good, I didn't need to go over to Torreys. I was spent. But it's less than a mile over to the other peak. It's right

If you can summit two peaks in one day, do it. JACOB PREBLE

there! And most importantly, I knew I didn't want to have to come back just to go a couple extra miles. So I started moving again and it was a bit of a slog for sure, but it was the right decision.

When you're ready to leave, take the trail that drops down in between the two peaks—this shortcut will reconnect with the Grays Peak Trail at 5.2 miles and you can then return the way you came.

Even with the best intentions, storms can build quickly and take you by surprise. Even if it's just cloudy, if you start to notice the hair on your arms (or head) standing up, lightning is building and you need to get out of there. If you find yourself stuck in a thunderstorm, get below treeline if you can and take shelter in a group of smaller, same-sized trees or by a large rock. Crouch with both feet firmly on the ground, 50 feet away from the next person and anything metal, like a walking pole, backpack with a metal frame, etc. Also be sure to bring layers, as the temperature can be drastically different at the peak than at the trailhead.

You'll often see mountain goats hanging out around the higher elevations. They may be curious, but never approach them, especially if they have young ones with them.

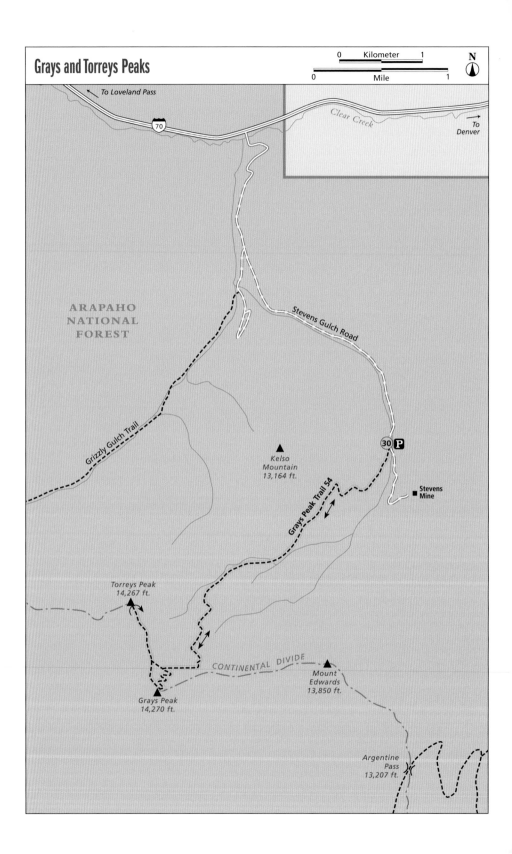

Grays and Torreys Peaks

To Loveland Pass

70

Clear Creek

To
Denver

Stevens Gulch Road

ARAPAHO
NATIONAL
FOREST

Grizzly Gulch Trail

Kelso
Mountain
13,164 ft.

30 P

Stevens
Mine

Grays Peak Trail 54

Torreys Peak
14,267 ft.

CONTINENTAL DIVIDE

Mount
Edwards
13,850 ft.

Grays Peak
14,270 ft.

Argentine
Pass
13,207 ft.

Miles and Directions

0.0 Start at the Grays Peak Trailhead.

1.5 Arrive at an informational sign and the climb begins.

1.8 Go straight to stay on the Grays Peak Trail.

2.7 Go left to summit Grays Peak.

3.5 Arrive at the top of Grays Peak (14,270 feet).

4.4 Hike across the saddle and arrive at the top of Torreys Peak (14,267 feet).

4.8 Depending on snow conditions, drop down on the trail between the two peaks to shortcut your way back.

5.2 Meet back up with the Grays Peak Trail and turn left back to the trailhead.

8.1 Arrive back at the trailhead.

Additional Route Options

There are no shorter routes, and you probably won't want to add anything on to this one. Enjoy your achievement!

31 South Park 600 Trail to Square Top Lakes

This is another hike that bumps right up to the Continental Divide at the far west reaches of the Front Range. Starting at the summit of Guanella Pass at 11,669 feet, this beautiful hike is entirely above the treeline. You'll be treated to views of Mount Bierstadt (14,065 feet), wildflowers upon wildflowers, and two alpine lakes. You can even tack on a peak summit if you'd like!

Start: South Park 600 Trailhead
Distance: 4.7 miles out and back
Difficulty: Moderately strenuous
Elevation gain: 945 feet
Hiking time: 2–3 hours
Trail surface: Dirt
Seasons/schedule: Summer to early fall
Fees and permits: None
Other trail users: Equestrians
Canine compatibility: Dogs must be on leash at all times.
Land status: Pike National Forest
Trail contact: South Platte Ranger District; (303) 275-5610; www.fs.usda.gov/recarea/psicc/recarea/?recid=12410

Maps: National Geographic Trails Illustrated #104: Idaho Springs/Loveland Pass
Nearest town: Georgetown
Cell service: None
Special considerations: If the parking lot is full, you can park along the road. Due to the popularity of the Mount Bierstadt Trail across the street, there may be limited parking in general on busy summer weekends. Guanella Pass typically opens the Friday before Memorial Day weekend and stays open through November, depending on the weather. The trail starts above 11,000 feet, so bring water and be prepared to bail on your hike if a storm is in the forecast.
Cell Service: None

Finding the trailhead: From the intersection of US 6 and I-25 in Denver, drive west on US 6 for 8.8 miles. Exit onto I-70 toward Grand Junction for 33 miles. Take exit 228 toward Georgetown and turn left onto 15th Street. At the traffic circle, take the first exit to turn right on Argentine Street for 0.5 mile. Turn left onto Sixth Street and then after 2 blocks, turn right onto Rose Street for 0.2 mile. Turn left onto Guanella Pass Road and follow this windy route 10.6 miles to the top. (During the fall, there are tons of places along this road worth stopping at to take in the aspens and fall colors.) When you get to the summit, there will be a large parking lot to your right. GPS: N39 35.85' / W105 42.75'

The Hike

The Guanella Pass Scenic Byway was first a burro trail then a wagon route in the 1860s, but wasn't officially named until 1953. It was then named after Byron Guanella, who had been a road supervisor and commissioner for Clear Creek County for nearly fifty years. The almost 24-mile road winds its way through the mountains to

The easy-to-follow trail gets a moderate rating due to the elevation and some climbing sections.

link the former mining town of Georgetown and I-70 with US 285. There are many trailheads and great hikes along the road, and I've seen moose more than once while driving.

The hike to Square Top Lakes starts at the summit parking lot at 11,669 feet. Take off across the alpine meadow. If you plan your trip in early to midsummer, you may catch the wildflowers in full bloom, bursting into reds, purples, and yellows.

The trail is very straightforward—there's only one way to go and only one intersecting trail. There is a creek crossing around 0.5 mile and the trail can be muddy, especially near the lakes. The only trail intersection you need to worry about is at 2 miles. It's between the two lakes, where the Square Top Trail branches off. You'll continue straight to the higher Square Top Lake.

On your way back, enjoy the views of Mount Bierstadt in the distance as you retrace your steps to the trailhead.

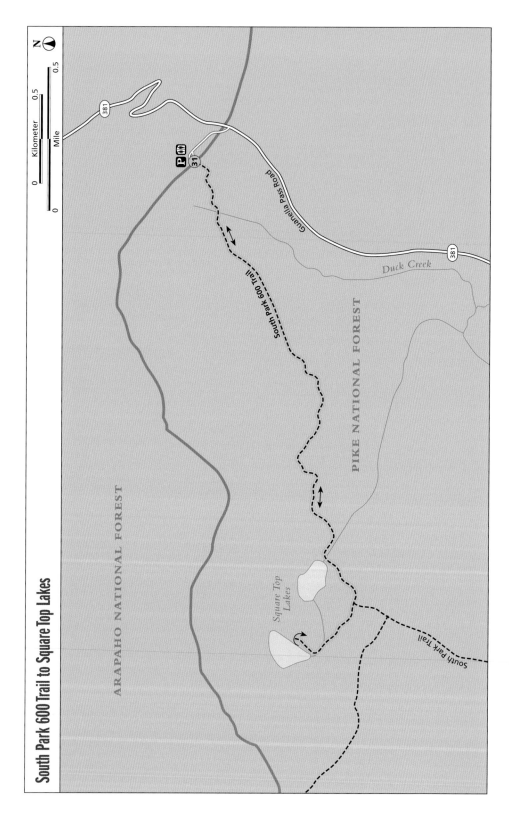

South Park 600 Trail to Square Top Lakes

N

Kilometer
0   0.5

Mile
0   0.5

ARAPAHO NATIONAL FOREST

PIKE NATIONAL FOREST

381

381

31

P

Guanella Pass Road

Duck Creek

South Park 600 Trail

Square Top Lakes

South Park Trail

This hike is great for views of wildflowers, mountains, and lakes.

Miles and Directions

0.0 Start at the South Park 600 Trailhead.

1.8 Arrive at the first Square Top Lake.

2.0 Stay straight to go to the second lake.

2.2 Arrive at the second Square Top Lake. Turn around and return the way you came.

4.7 Arrive back at the trailhead.

Additional Route Options

Tack on a peak and take the left at 2 miles to stay on the South Park Trail. At 2.8 miles, turn right and follow the ridge until you summit Square Top Mountain (13,794) at 4 miles. Turn around and come back the way you came.

32 Castlewood Canyon State Park Loops

Tucked away east of Castle Rock, Castlewood Canyon State Park offers visitors a glimpse of Denver's history, featuring grassy plains that lead to rugged cliffs and a narrow ravine carved by Cherry Creek over millions of years. Drop down to the water past chunks of Castle Rock conglomerate to see what's left of the old dam that burst and flooded the city in 1933.

Start: Lake Gulch Trailhead at Canyon Point
Distance: 6.2-mile figure eight
Difficulty: Moderate
Elevation gain: 731 feet
Hiking time: 2-3 hours
Trail surface: Dirt with some rocky sections
Seasons/schedule: Year-round. The park is open from sunrise to sunset.
Fees and permits: Daily entrance fee or annual state parks pass required
Other trail users: None
Canine compatibility: Dogs must be on leash at all times.

Land status: Castlewood Canyon State Park
Trail contact: Castlewood Canyon State Park; (303) 688-5242; https://cpw.state.co.us/placestogo/parks/CastlewoodCanyon/Pages/default.aspx
Maps: Castlewood Canyon State Park map
Nearest town: Franktown
Cell service: Good at trailhead; may be spotty on trail
Special considerations: This trail is very exposed, so avoid hot summer days.

Finding the trailhead: From the intersection of US 6 and I-25 in Denver, drive south on I-25 for 24.7 miles. Use the right two lanes to take exit 184 for US 85 N/Meadows Parkway toward CO 86 E/Founders Parkway. Turn left on Meadows Parkway for 0.2 mile and then continue on to CO 86/Founders Parkway for 4.2 miles. Turn left on CO 86 for 5 miles, then turn right onto CO 83 and follow it for 5 miles to the park entrance. Drive to the last parking lot at Canyon Point. GPS: N39 20.01' / W104 44.77'

The Hike

On this hike, you'll see what's left of the old dam, originally built in 1890 across Cherry Creek. There was a reservoir on the north side of the dam that was a very popular spot for Denverites to camp, canoe, and fish. After several days of heavy rain in 1933, the water level rose above the dam and caused it to burst on August 3, sending fast-moving waves of water toward Denver. The dam tender was able to warn the Denver Police Department and some Cherry Creek residents, so the surge only caused two fatalities but could have been much worse.

> This trail is fully exposed, so be sure to bring water and don't set out for your hike during the hottest part of the day.

See the remains of the dam that once spanned the entire canyon.

The Lake Gulch Trail starts with a view of Pikes Peak and then winds down slabs of the Castle Rock Conglomerate, formed millions of years ago. Once you connect with the Rimrock Trail, you'll have views of the dam ruins, as well as the green fields where the reservoir once was. There are some patches of trees along this part of the trail, including ponderosa pine and juniper, and then plants such as mountain mahogany, prickly pear, yucca, and Gambel oak, but there isn't much shade along this trail.

Once you drop down along the creek, look for smoke marks in the caves and overhangs, evidence of the Indigenous nomadic people who moved through the area 5,000 years ago. It's also likely that the Mouache Ute called Castlewood Canyon

On clear days you can see all the way to Pikes Peak from the amphitheater at the beginning of this hike.

home at one time, taking advantage of the available shelter and water in the area to make winters more tolerable.

Just after 4 miles, the Falls Spur Trail will come in. You can take this side adventure or continue on to where the trail curves to the left and still get a look at the falls without getting off-course. Continue along the cottonwood-lined creek and get a closer look at the towering dam ruins.

At 5 miles, you'll come to a junction with two other trails. Turn right to climb out of the canyon on the Inner Canyon Trail. Be cautious of rattlesnakes in the rockier sections as you make your way out of the canyon and back to the trailhead. Follow the Inner Canyon Trail back to the Canyon View Nature Trail. Take a right and then finish the loop back at the trailhead.

Castlewood Canyon State Park Loops

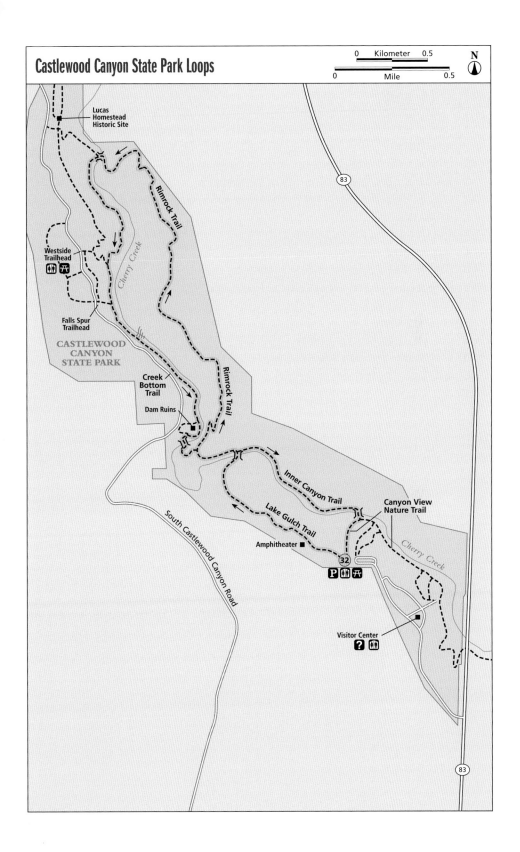

0 — Kilometer — 0.5
0 — Mile — 0.5

N

Lucas Homestead Historic Site

Rimrock Trail

83

Cherry Creek

Westside Trailhead

Falls Spur Trailhead

CASTLEWOOD CANYON STATE PARK

Creek Bottom Trail

Dam Ruins

Rimrock Trail

Inner Canyon Trail

Lake Gulch Trail

Canyon View Nature Trail

Cherry Creek

Amphitheater

32

P

South Castlewood Canyon Road

Visitor Center

?

83

Miles and Directions

0.0 Start at the Lake Gulch Trailhead.

0.2 Continue straight past the spur trail.

0.9 Come to the junction of the Lake Gulch and Inner Canyon Trails; go left and up the wooden steps.

1.1 Come to a trail junction and stay right to get on the Rimrock Trail.

1.3 Take a sharp right (there is a cairn marking the switchback).

3.2 Cross the bridge over Cherry Creek and come to a trail junction; turn left onto the Creek Bottom Trail.

3.9 Come to a junction with the Westside Trailhead; turn left and walk down the wooden steps.

4.1 Continue straight to stay on the Creek Bottom Trail.

4.8 Continue straight to stay on the Creek Bottom Trail.

5.0 Come to a trail junction; turn right onto the Inner Canyon Trail.

5.2 Come to a junction with the Inner Canyon and Lake Gulch Trails; continue straight onto the Inner Canyon Trail.

5.5 Continue straight to stay on the Inner Canyon Trail.

6.0 Turn right onto the Canyon View Nature Trail.

6.2 Arrive back at the trailhead.

Additional Route Options

There are two different spur trails that you can take to walk around the dam ruins (4.8 miles) or stop by the falls (4.1 miles).

33 South Rim and Willow Creek Trails— Roxborough State Park

Roxborough State Park covers 4,000 acres southwest of Denver and has some really impressive red rock formations. The South Rim and Willow Creek Trails wind through the trees and creek along the bottom of the valley, come up through a meadow, then climb to the rim for some of the best views in the park. There isn't much tree coverage on the South Rim Trail, so this is a wonderful sunset hike in the summer.

Start: Willow Creek Trailhead
Distance: 2.8-mile loop
Difficulty: Easy
Elevation gain: 417 feet
Hiking time: 1–1.5 hours
Trail surface: Dirt
Seasons/schedule: Year-round. Hours vary but the park is typically open from 7 a.m. to 9 p.m. in the summer and 8 a.m. to 5 p.m. in the winter.
Fees and permits: Daily entrance fee or annual state parks pass required
Other trail users: None
Canine compatibility: No dogs allowed
Land status: Roxborough State Park

Trail contact: Roxborough State Park; (303) 973-3959; https://cpw.state.co.us/places togo/parks/Roxborough/Pages/default.aspx
Maps: Roxborough State Park map
Nearest town: Highlands Ranch
Cell service: Good
Special considerations: Park hours vary by season; check the website or call the park for more information. No pets, drones, camping, mountain bikes, horses, rock climbing, fires, or marijuana are permitted in Roxborough State Park. The park can get very busy on summer weekends and holidays between 10 a.m. and 2 p.m. If the parking lot is full, you will be denied entry and there is no other parking nearby.

Finding the trailhead: From the intersection of US 6 and I-25 in Denver, drive south on I-25 for 1.3 miles. Use the right two lanes to take exit 207B for US 85 toward Santa Fe Drive for 14.4 miles. Take the Titan Parkway exit, then turn right onto Titan Parkway and continue to West Titan Road for 0.8 mile. At the traffic circle, take the second exit to stay on West Titan Road. Keep right to stay on West Titan Road for 1.8 miles, then continue to North Rampart Range Road for 3.8 miles. Turn left onto Roxborough Drive (if you miss the turn, you'll go straight into a gated neighborhood), then take an immediate right to continue on Roxborough. Drive 2.1 miles to the end of the road and park near the visitor center. GPS: N39 25.74' / W105 04.11'

The Hike

After parking near the visitor center, I highly recommend taking a walk through the building if it's open, or at least walking past the building and taking a look at the flower garden. Check out the labels and learn more about the plants that you will likely see along this hike. From there, walk across the dirt road to the Willow Creek Trailhead southwest of the visitor center. The Fountain Valley Trail follows the wide

Get a look at the park's red rock formations as you come to the meadow on the Willow Creek Trail.

road to the north, and the Willow Creek Trail is a more narrow route into the trees. There will be a sign at the trailhead noting the conditions and whether the trail is muddy, dry, etc.

The trail immediately heads downhill through a shady, wet habitat. As you wind your way through here, keep an eye out for deer hiding among the tall grasses and listen for the birds. Once you reach the meadow, you'll also see the park's red rock formation across the way. At 0.5 mile, the trail splits and you start to climb on the South Rim Trail.

Once called Washington Park by homesteaders who thought the rock outcroppings looked like George Washington—and not to be confused with the Washington Park in the city of Denver—Roxborough State Park has long been a special place for locals. Between the prehistoric rock shelters and campsites dating back to at least the Early Archaic period (5500–3000 BCE) and the rock formations from millions of years ago, the park is rich in geologic and cultural history. As the Denver metropolitan area pushed farther south, it became clear that this area needed to be protected. Besides its designation as a state park, Roxborough is also a Colorado Natural Area, a

> Be sure to stay on the trail to minimize your impact on this carefully protected land.

Stop by the garden at the visitor center to learn about native plants like the showy milkweed, which plays an important role for butterflies and bees.

The view to the northwest coming down the South Rim Trail.

National Natural Landmark, a National Archeological District, an Audubon Important Bird Area, and a Leave No Trace Gold Standard Designated Site.

As you work your way up to the ridge, there is a bench under a lovely tree and then at 1.5 miles a short spur trail that leads to a bench overlooking a meadow. It's behind some trees and quite peaceful. The best views are after you top out on the ridge and start to come back down, especially if you're hiking during sunset.

Continue your descent back into the oak trees to reconnect with the Willow Creek Trail. Cross a bridge and follow the trail north past the restrooms and across the park road. Turn left on the trail on the other side of the road and follow it back through two parking lots to your original starting point.

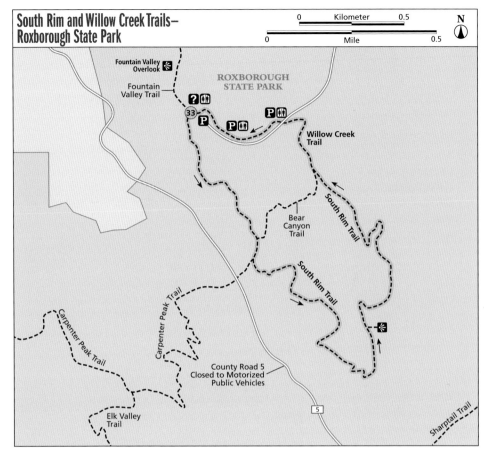

Miles and Directions

0.0 Start at the Willow Creek Trailhead.

0.5 Come to a junction with the Bear Canyon Trail; turn right.

0.6 Turn left onto the South Rim Trail.

1.2 It appears that the trail splits, but it does not; stay to the right on the main trail.

1.5 Arrive at the top of the ridge; check out the scenic viewpoint on the right.

2.4 Reconnect with the Willow Creek Trail; go straight and cross bridge.

2.6 Arrive at restrooms and a parking lot; cross the park road and turn left on the trail on the other side.

2.8 Arrive back at the trailhead.

Additional Route Options

From the visitor center, hike the Fountain Valley Loop before Willow Creek and South Rim to add 2.7 miles and almost double your distance. This loop has even more forma-tion views and stops by the Henry Persse homestead, built in the early 1900s.

34 Sandstone Meadow Loop

I recently discovered the Sandstone Ranch Open Space, and while there are only two trail options here, it's a real gem. Butting up to Pike National Forest, the options here overlook meadows, rocky formations, and historic ranching operations while winding through wildlife—and not-so-wild animal—habitats.

Start: Sandstone Ranch Open Space trailhead
Distance: 4.6-mile loop
Difficulty: Easy
Elevation gain: 417 feet
Hiking time: 1.5–2 hours
Trail surface: Dirt
Seasons/schedule: Year-round. The trailhead is open 1 hour before sunrise to 1 hour after sunset.
Fees and permits: None
Other trail users: Equestrians and mountain bikers
Canine compatibility: Dogs must be on leash at all times.

Land status: Douglas County Open Space
Trail contact: Douglas County Open Space; (303) 660-7495; www.douglas.co.us/open-space- natural-resources/properties/sandstone-ranch
Maps: Sandstone Ranch Open Space map
Nearest town: Larkspur
Cell service: Good
Special considerations: A good part of the trail is exposed, so it can get very warm (but this is also what makes it a great hike in the winter/spring!). Hike in the morning or evening during the summer and bring plenty of water.

Finding the trailhead: From the intersection of US 6 and I-25 in Denver, drive south on I-25 for 36.7 miles. Take exit 173 toward Larkspur, then continue onto South Spruce Mountain Road for 1.3 miles. Turn right onto East Perry Park Avenue for 3.2 miles, then turn left onto CO 105 for 0.7 mile. Turn left into the Sandstone Ranch Open Space parking lot. GPS: N39 13.44' / W104 56.14'

The Hike

There are two main trails at the Sandstone Ranch Open Space and they go in opposite directions. The Sandstone Meadow Loop starts at the west end of the parking lot, south of the restrooms and the picnic pavilion. Take a right to follow the loop counterclockwise. Most of the first 1 to 1.5 miles is winding your way up through a forested area to the overlook. This section is also curvy and mountain bikers won't have the best visibility, so pay attention to your surroundings through here. From the overlook, you'll have nice views of the Pike National Forest and some of the rock formations. Continue on the Sandstone Meadow Loop until 1.5 miles, where you'll turn left and walk 0.4 mile to the Ranch Overlook.

The Sandstone Ranch Open Space is a relatively new recreation area. Douglas County purchased the land in 2018, protecting the land that supports multiple ecosystems and is home to a rare mouse species and a rare plant species. The Preble's

The first part of the trail passes through a forested area.

meadow jumping mouse was first documented in Colorado in 1899 and hasn't been seen in Denver, Adams, or Arapahoe Counties since at least 1991. It's believed that urban development has pushed the mouse out of its habitats and so the animal has been categorized as threatened on the federal endangered and threatened species list since 1998. A few years ago, the extremely rare white marsh bellflower was spotted along Gove Ditch, along with several other uncommon plants.

It's not just the plants and wildlife that make this hike interesting—there's a great variety in the rocks around you too. The red sandstone formations are part of the Fountain Formation from the Pennsylvanian period, dating back about 300 million years, while the mountains in the background are closer to 1 billion years old. There are also rocks from the Cambrian, Ordovician, and Mississippian periods—all hundreds of millions of years old.

As you finish out the loop, you'll walk through active grazing lands and may come across some cows. The cows will stare at you and definitely aren't in any hurry to move away like wildlife would be. While it's unlikely that a cow would charge, they can be territorial when babies are around, so it's better to give them as much room as possible and keep your dogs and young children close.

Unique rock formations can be seen throughout this hike.

Miles and Directions

0.0 Start at the trailhead on the west side of the parking lot.

0.2 Turn right onto the Sandstone Meadow Loop.

0.7 Arrive at an overlook.

0.9 Come to a junction with the Crooked Stick Connector Trail; continue straight.

1.5 Come to a junction with the Ranch Overlook Trail; turn right.

1.9 Arrive at the Ranch Overlook. When you're done here, retrace your steps and turn right to continue on the Sandstone Meadow Loop.

2.9 Come to a junction with the Sunset Ridge Trail; stay to the right.

3.8 Pass through a metal gate.

3.9 Come to a second junction with the Sunset Ridge Trail; stay to the right.

4.4 Turn right to return to the trailhead.

4.6 Arrive back at the trailhead.

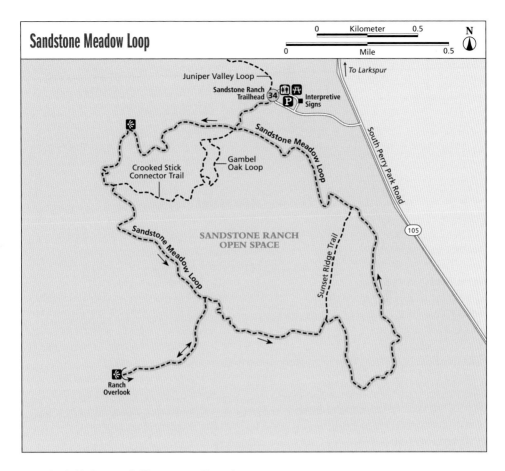

Sandstone Meadow Loop

Additional Route Options

For a longer hike, add on the 3.4-mile Juniper Valley Loop through the other side of the open space. To cut your hike short, take a left on the Sunset Ridge Trail at 2.9 miles. This will cut a little over 0.5 mile from your total distance.

35 Devil's Head Lookout Trail

This fun hike isn't too long or too difficult and has informational signs throughout, making it a great option for families, although you may want to keep kids close if you take the 140-plus steps to the top of the Devil's Head Lookout Tower. The tower has been in use since 1912 and it's the only full-time fire lookout left in Colorado. Depending on when you go, you might catch a glimpse of the tower's working cats, Fiona and Fjord.

Start: Devil's Head Trailhead
Distance: 2.8 miles out and back
Difficulty: Moderate
Elevation gain: 495 feet
Hiking time: 1.5–2 hours
Trail surface: Dirt and rock
Seasons/schedule: Late spring through summer
Fees and permits: None
Other trail users: None
Canine compatibility: Dogs must be on leash at all times.
Land status: Rampart Range Recreation Area
Trail contact: South Platte Ranger District; (303) 275-5610; www.fs.usda.gov/recarea/psicc/recarea/?recid=12410
Maps: National Geographic Trails Illustrated #135: Deckers/Rampart Range

Nearest town: Sedalia
Cell service: None
Special considerations: The lookout tower deck is open to the public when it is staffed, which is typically late May through early September. The parking area is open from 1 hour before sunrise to 1 hour after sunset. The roads and trails in this area close by December 1 (sometimes earlier) and remain closed through the winter. The Forest Service tries to reopen by April 1, but roads and trails may remain closed until late May depending on the weather. This is a popular hike. If the main parking lot is full, there are some obvious places to park along the road on the 0.5 mile leading up to the trailhead.

Finding the trailhead: From the intersection of US 6 and I-25 in Denver, drive south on I-25 for 21.9 miles. Take exit 187 for Happy Canyon Road and turn right onto East Happy Canyon Road for 0.9 mile. At the traffic circle, go straight to stay on East Happy Canyon Road for 1.1 miles. At the next traffic circle, continue straight onto West Happy Canyon Road for 0.2 mile. Turn right onto US 85 for 3.1 miles, then use the two left lanes to stay on US 85 for 0.1 mile. Turn left onto CO 67 for 10 miles, then turn left onto the unpaved Rampart Range Road for 8.9 miles. When the road splits, continue straight until you reach a dead end at the trailhead. GPS: N39 16.17' / W105 06.31'

The Hike

Even though this is a family-friendly hike, most of the trail is uphill on your way to the lookout, so it may be slow going depending on the age and activity level of your family members. That being said, there are some beautiful views, benches and

If you're afraid of heights, you may just want to view the lookout from the ground.

picnic tables, and informational signs along the way that offer plenty of opportunities for a break.

The trail starts at the south end of the parking lot, and you'll make your way uphill along a gully of downed trees. While tornadoes are uncommon in Colorado, they happen, and one blew through here on July 21, 2015. It was rated an EF1, which means estimated winds of 86 to 110 miles per hour. Continue through an aspen grove and a little creek.

As the route winds its way toward the lookout through the forest, you'll start to notice huge boulders on the sides of the trail that range in color from light pink to reddish. These rocks are made of Pikes Peak granite, formed over 1 billion years ago and originating at Pikes Peak 30 miles

In 1919, Helen Dowe became the first female fire lookout in the United States, spending three seasons as a lookout at Devil's Head.

The grainy pink rock that makes up the boulders along the trail is Pikes Peak granite.

south. The pinkish color comes from large amounts of microcline feldspar and iron minerals found in the rock.

A couple climber trails (well marked) and the Zinn Trail will cross your path. You'll come across the Zinn Trail at 1.2 miles, and you'll just continue to the right. When you get to the top of the Devil's Head Lookout Trail, there are still some 140 steps to visit the lookout. If you are afraid of heights, you might want to just view it from the bottom. The metal steps are very secure and there's room for two single-file lines, but it can make you feel a little squirmy. At the top, a limited number of people are allowed on the lookout at one time. Again, it's very secure and there is a railing all the way around, but you can feel pretty exposed. If there is lightning or the threat of lightning in the area, the staircase will be closed.

Run by the US Forest Service, the Devil's Head Lookout is the last of the four original Front Range fire lookout towers that is still in use and was added to the National Historic Lookout Register in 1990. The people who work at the tower use binoculars to spot fires while they are small, then use the Osbourne Firefinder

The stairs are secure but might be a little uncomfortable for someone who is afraid of heights.

to determine the exact location of the fire and call it in so that it can be managed. The tower calls in an average of three to seven fires per summer, depending on the weather. In the summer of 2023, for example, there were five small fires in a single week in July, one caused by a human and the other four resulting from lightning.

On clear days, you can see for 100 miles in every direction from the lookout's perch at 9,748 feet. Look for Denver to the north, Kansas to the east, Pikes Peak to the south, and the Continental Divide to the west.

Miles and Directions

0.0 Start at the Devil's Head Trailhead.

0.6 The trail runs into a boulder; take a sharp left.

0.9 Continue left and uphill.

1.2 Come to a junction with the Zinn Trail; turn right.

1.4 Arrive at Devil's Head Lookout. Return the way you came.

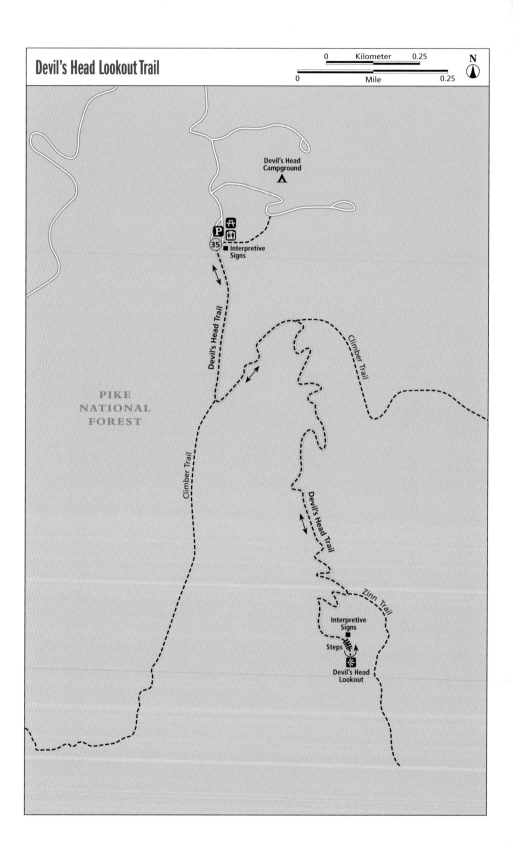

Devil's Head Lookout Trail

0   Kilometer   0.25

0   Mile   0.25

N

Devil's Head
Campground

P
35
■ Interpretive
Signs

Devil's Head Trail

Climber Trail

PIKE
NATIONAL
FOREST

Climber Trail

Devil's Head Trail

Zinn Trail

Interpretive
Signs
■
Steps

Devil's Head
Lookout

Even on cloudy days, you'll have views for miles.

2.1 There is a section here that is a mix of wooden steps and cement with metal rein-
forcements. It's grippy on the way up but felt a little slippery on the way down, so be
careful here.

2.8 Arrive back at trailhead.

Additional Route Options

There aren't any connecting trails here; the Zinn Trail is just a different, shorter out-
and-back trail to get to the lookout. There are some spur trails for climbing access.

Bonus Hikes at a Glance

E. O'Fallon Park Loop

This park is tucked along a bend in Bear Creek, offering mountain views from the West Ridge Loop and a peaceful meadow on the Bear Creek Trail. This is one of those places where you'll have moments of feelings like you are out in the middle of nowhere, when you're really just a few minutes away from the closest town. For a moderate 3.7-mile outing, start at the West Ridge parking lot off CO 74 and take the steeper, rockier West Ridge Loop around to the Bear Creek Trail. (There is a good amount of parking, but the park can get busy on the weekends, so if that parking lot is full, take Myers Gulch Road over to the Pence Park trailhead.) The West Ridge Loop is hiking only, but the Bear Creek Loop is open to mountain bikers and equestrians. Bring your four-legged hiking buddy on this one, but they have to stay on a leash.

Purple aspen daisies are a popular wildflower along the Front Range.

Finding the trailhead: From the intersection of US 6 and I-25 in Denver, drive west on US 6 for 8.8 miles. Take the exit onto I-70 toward Grand Junction and continue on I-70 for 1 mile. Use the right two lanes to take exit 260 for CO 470 toward Colorado Springs. Merge onto CO 470 east and continue for 3.8 miles. Take exit 4 for CO 8/Morrison Road. Follow this for 0.4 mile, and then it will merge with Bear Creek Avenue. Continue straight for 7.7 miles, then turn left onto Lines Lane and follow it to the parking lot. GPS: N39 39.33' / W105 17.36

F. Bergen Peak

If you're looking for a more strenuous climb without having to go into the mountains, Bergen Peak fits the bill. This hike steadily climbs through the forest in Elk Meadow Park, gaining over 2,000 feet in elevation on your way to 9,708 feet. There are some steep sections, especially the switchbacks toward the top, but panoramic views in every direction. In the late spring through midsummer there are beautiful wildflowers at the beginning of this popular trail. Dogs are not allowed, and you'll likely see other hikers and mountain bikers on the way. This is a popular trail, so getting there earlier is better. From the parking lot, go north on the Sleep "S" Trail. Take a left on the Meadow View Trail at 0.3 mile and then another left on the Bergen Peak Trail at 0.9 mile. At 3.6 miles, you'll drop down to a junction with the Too Long Trail; turn left and push through the switchbacks to the top.

Finding the trailhead: From the intersection of US 6 and I-25 in Denver, drive west on US 6 for 8.8 miles. Take the exit onto I-70 toward Grand Junction and continue on I-70 for 9.3 miles. Use the right two lanes to take exit 252 for CO 74 toward Evergreen Parkway for 0.6 mile, then continue straight onto CO 74 for 4.5 miles. Turn right onto Bergen Peak Drive, take a quick right, and then another right into the Elk Meadow parking lot. GPS: N39 39.78' / W105 21.52'

Colorado Springs Area

Colorado Springs is a lot of things, depending on who you're talking to. It's home to the Colorado Springs Olympic & Paralympic Training Center for Team USA athletes. There's a significant military presence with the United States Air Force Academy, Fort Carson, Peterson Air Force Base, and Schriever Air Force Base all located here. There's also the Cheyenne Mountain Complex, which plays a vital role in early warning and defense against missile threats, including nuclear ones. It is designed to withstand a nuclear blast and offers secure communication and command facilities.

The area also plays host to one of the oldest motorsport events in the United States: the Pikes Peak International Hill Climb, an annual automobile race that runs 12.4 miles with 156 turns up the 14,115-foot peak. There's also the Pikes Peak Ascent, a 13.3-mile footrace from Manitou Springs to the summit of Pikes Peak. Swiss runner Rèmi Bonnet just broke the thirty-year record in 2023 with a time of 2:01:06. Pikes Peak is also open to us mere mortals in regular ol' cars. There's a fee to drive up the road, but the view is breathtaking (literally)—so much so that Katharine Lee Bates was inspired to write "America the Beautiful" after visiting the summit.

And, of course, we can't forget about the Manitou Incline, a stairway made of railroad ties that covers a vertical gain of approximately 2,000 feet in just under a mile (that's a 68 percent average grade). Bonnet also set that record, in 2022, with a time of 17 minutes and 25 seconds.

In short, Colorado Springs is a town built for adventure and inspiration. There are a dozen natural areas and open spaces in and around the Springs, with trails for hikers, runners, cyclists, and equestrians. The trails in this section represent something for everyone and highlight some of the best of the best. From a walk through a wildlife area to a hike in the hills, hopefully the selected trails make you want to see what else is out there waiting for you to discover.

Garden of the Gods is just as iconic for Colorado Springs as Red Rocks Park and Amphitheatre is for Denver. JACOB PREBLE

36 Paint Mines Interpretive Park

This one is technically a tad east and into the plains for the Front Range, but it's such a unique and one-of-a-kind place, it had to have an entry in this guide. The park is named after the colorful clays that Indigenous people once used to make paint, dating back as far as 9,000 years ago. From bright pink and purple to peach and orange, the colored bands are caused by oxidized iron compounds. The bands wrap around spires and hoodoos, and a walk on this 4-mile trail will feel like you've stepped into another world.

Start: Paint Mines Interpretive Park trailhead
Distance: 4-mile figure eight
Difficulty: Easy
Elevation gain: 450 feet
Hiking time: 2-3 hours, depending on how much time you spend exploring the formations
Trail surface: Dirt
Seasons/schedule: Year-round. The park is open from dawn to dusk.
Fees and permits: None
Other trail users: None
Canine compatibility: No dogs allowed
Land status: El Paso County Parks
Trail contact: El Paso County Parks; (970) 520-6375; https://communityservices .elpasoco.com/parks-and-recreation/ paint-mines-interpretive-park

Maps: USGS Calhan and Paint Mines Interpretive Park Trail Map (available online)
Nearest town: Calhan
Cell service: None
Special considerations: Mornings and evenings are the best times to see the colors on full display. The formations are very fragile; as such, dogs, horses, and bicycles are prohibited. Entering, climbing, or scrambling in or on the formations is prohibited. Drones are prohibited. Do not remove, destroy, or disturb any plants, rocks, minerals, wildlife, or artifacts that you may find. Be careful if there has been recent rain, as it can get muddy, and beware of flash flooding if rain is in the forecast. The trail is also completely exposed and can get very hot on a sunny day, so bring water with you.

Finding the trailhead: From the intersection of I-25 and South Nevada Avenue (CO 115) in Colorado Springs, take I-25 south for 0.3 mile. Use the right two lanes to take exit 139 for US 24 east toward Airport/Limon. Continue on US 24 for 4.1 miles, then use the left two lanes to stay on US 24 for 2.1 miles. Take exit 141 to merge onto US 24/East Platte Avenue. After 1 mile, keep left to continue on US 24 for 28.2 miles. Turn right on Yoder Street for 0.7 mile. Turn left onto Paint Mine Road for 1.4 miles until you get to the parking lot on your left. GPS: N39 01.32' / W104 16.44'

The Hike

The Paint Mines that we see today are the result of millions and millions of years of geologic processes. Fifty-five million years ago, this part of Colorado was a tropical rainforest. The forest and soils were covered by white sandstone from Pikes Peak granite. Over time, unforgiving prairie wind and rain eroded the stone and clay, revealing the gullies and hoodoos (spires) that exist today. The human history of the

The overlooks give you a bird's-eye view of the colorful formations.

park dates back as far as 9,000 years ago when Apache, Arapahoe, Cheyenne, Comanche, Kiowa, and Ute people used the clay to make pottery and the colors to make paint. Before settlers arrived, Indigenous people hunted bison, caribou, and deer here. Today, the park is home to pronghorn antelope, mule deer, coyotes, raccoons, skunks, rabbits, burrowing rodents, a variety of birds, and some frogs and lizards.

When the town of Calhan started developing in the late 1880s/early 1890s, the clay was mined and used to make fire brick, pottery, and tile. In fact, several buildings in Colorado Springs and Pueblo were constructed from bricks made with Paint Mines clay. People later used the area for picnics, Easter services, and partying. In 1997, El Paso County started purchasing the land to preserve it, and the interpretive park opened in June 2005.

After reading the interpretive signs in the parking lot, make your way straight down to a dry creek bed. Avoid this part of the trail during wet weather. Follow the figure eight around to see the hoodoos, unusual and somewhat whimsical spires with colorful bands and a large boulder sitting on top. At 1.8 miles there will be one of very few benches on this trail and an overlook of the hoodoos. Another example of these colorful formations can be found in Bryce Canyon National Park in Utah.

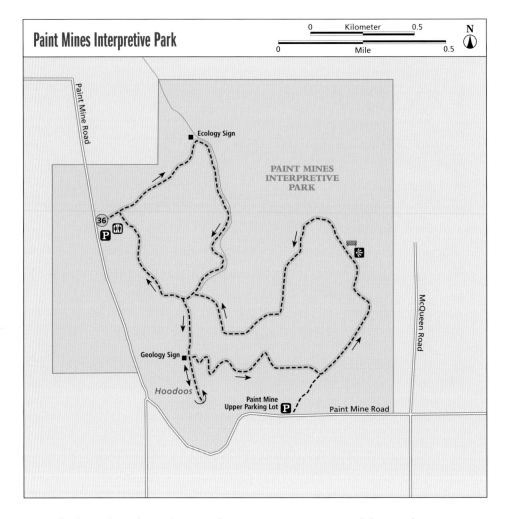

Paint Mines Interpretive Park

Walk along the ridge and notice the prairie grasses, cacti, and flowers that some-how thrive in what appears to be a harsh environment. Seeing the formations from above gives you a really interesting perspective on the forces of nature and how pow-erful wind and water can be.

Miles and Directions

0.0 Start at the Paint Mines Interpretive Park trailhead.

0.4 The low point of the hike is just after the ecology sign. This section is especially slippery when wet.

1.1 Come to the X junction and continue straight.

1.3 Continue straight to the geology interpretive sign. Do not take the social trails here; go straight ahead 0.2 mile down the gully, then turn around and come back.

1.7 Turn right.

It's not all bright colors—there are some lighter-colored rocks here too (although they can be blinding in the sun thanks to the quartzite!).

1.8 Arrive at an overlook.

2.3 Come to a junction with a trail to the other parking lot; continue left.

3.6 Come back to the X junction and go straight.

3.7 Arrive at a scenic viewpoint.

3.9 Turn left.

4.0 Arrive back at the trailhead.

Additional Route Options

The only other option is to drive a little farther down the road and drop in from the Upper Parking Lot, but it doesn't change anything about the hike.

37 Lost Pond Loop—Mueller State Park

Mueller State Park is one of the lesser-visited parks in the system, but has some wonderful hiking options. More than 50 miles of trails wind through the park, including 34 miles of trails for horseback riding and 36 miles for mountain biking. There are more than a hundred campsites and backcountry camping options, too. The Lost Pond Loop is an easy hike with a couple of steep sections that goes through the forest, past two ponds, and includes some great views before climbing back up to the trailhead.

Start: Lost Pond Trailhead
Distance: 2.8-mile loop
Difficulty: Easy-moderate
Elevation gain: 433 feet
Hiking time: 1–1.5 hours
Trail surface: Dirt
Seasons/schedule: Year-round. Day-use hours are 5 a.m. to 10 p.m.
Fees and permits: Daily entrance fee or annual state parks pass required

Other trail users: Mountain bikers on some parts of the loop
Canine compatibility: No dogs allowed
Land status: Mueller State Park
Trail contact: Mueller State Park; (719) 687-2366; https://cpw.state.co.us/placestogo/parks/Mueller
Maps: Mueller State Park map
Nearest town: Divide
Cell service: None
Special considerations: None

Finding the trailhead: From the intersection of I-25 and West Cimarron Street (US 24), go west on US 24 for 25 miles. Turn left onto CO 67 south for 3.9 miles. Turn right onto Wapiti (Elk) Road into the state park entrance and then continue for 0.9 mile until you get to the Lost Pond Trailhead on your left. There will be a sign pointing you in the right direction. GPS: N38 53.10' / W105 10.93'

The Hike

The land that is now Mueller State Park was once the hunting grounds of the Ute people. Homesteaders, ranchers, and farmers had taken over the area by the 1860s and then thousands of people flocked here after gold was discovered in 1900. W. E. Mueller bought ten of the ranches and homesteads to create Mueller Ranch, and in the 1980s the ranch was used as a game preserve. After the Nature Conservancy and Colorado Parks & Wildlife purchased the land, it was turned into the state park and opened in 1988.

Considered one of the most overlooked state parks in Colorado, it's easy to

> Black bears are often seen in the park in the spring, summer, and fall. Strict food storage regulations apply year-round; visit the park website for details.

The trail's namesake pond.

find solitude out here. The Lost Pond Loop starts at the trailhead of the same name. Walk downhill and turn right. You'll soon come to a trail junction; turn left to follow the loop clockwise. There are wildflowers of all colors sprinkled along the path—white, purple, yellow, blue, and red—as you walk down the gravely trail. Logging efforts cleared out some of the trees along the trail, but aspens grew in their place, making this a lovely and peaceful fall hike. Lost Pond is just 0.5 mile along the trail on your left and frequented by dragonflies and tiger salamanders. Take the path around the pond for a mini-loop and then continue on the Geer Pond Trail.

Turn right at 1 mile. At 1.2 miles, you'll pass Geer Pond and take a right onto the Beaver Ponds Trail. Here, you'll drop down in the valley and along a creek. At 1.6 miles, turn right onto the Homestead Trail to climb a rocky, pine forest section. When you're almost at the top, you'll come to a junction with four trails. Turn right onto Reveneur's Ridge and follow this back to close the loop. Finish out the hike the way you came.

Lost Pond Loop—Mueller State Park

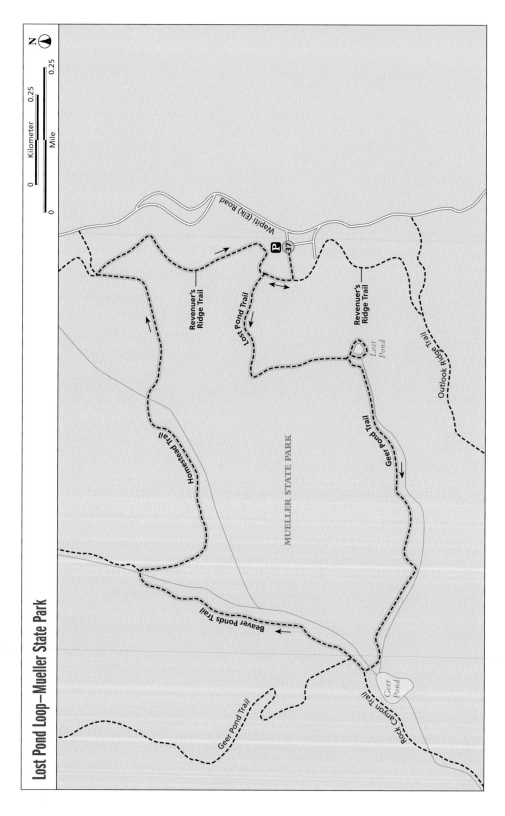

Revenuer's Ridge Trail

Lost Pond Trail

Wapiti (Elk) Road

P
37

Revenuer's Ridge Trail

Lost Pond

Outlook Ridge Trail

Homestead Trail

Geer Pond Trail

MUELLER STATE PARK

Beaver Ponds Trail

Geer Pond Trail

Geer Pond

Rock Canyon Trail

N

Kilometer
0   0.25

Mile
0   0.25

Be sure to stop by the covered scenic overlook in the visitor center parking lot and check out the interpretive sign to find the three highest peaks in the state (Mount Elbert, Mount Massive, and Mount Harvard).

Miles and Directions

0.0 Start at the Lost Pond Trailhead and turn right. In 500 feet, turn left to start the Lost Pond Loop.

0.5 Arrive at Lost Pond. Continue west on the Geer Pond Trail.

1.0 Turn right to stay on the Geer Pond Trail.

1.2 Turn right onto the Beaver Ponds Trail.

1.6 Turn right onto the Homestead Trail.

2.3 Come to a junction with four trails; turn right onto Reveneur's Ridge.

2.7 Turn left. In 500 feet, turn left again.

2.8 Arrive back at the trailhead.

Additional Route Options

Several other trails in the area intersect with this trail. Pick up a trail map at the visitor center before you head out to map your route.

ENCOUNTERS WITH NATURE: BLACK BEARS

Black bears can be found all over the mountains in Colorado. Measuring 5 to 6 feet from head to tail and weighing 150 to 350 pounds, they are the smallest bears found in North America. Black is a species, not a color, and these bears can be blonde, cinnamon, or brown. Bears have a sense of smell that is a hundred times more sensitive than humans, which is why it's so important to know and follow food storage practices. Once bears find food, they will come back, and this may lead to the destruction of the bear by Colorado Parks & Wildlife.

If you are hiking in bear country, never hike alone and always let someone know where you are going. Stay on designated trails and make noise when approaching blind corners, water, or a dense forest area. A bear's first instinct is to stay away from any perceived danger, but if you do encounter a black bear:

- Stay calm.
- Leave the area if the bear hasn't yet noticed you.
- If the bear does see you, back away slowly. Do not run.
- Speak softly or not at all. Do not yell.
- Stand your ground if the bear charges you—they are usually bluffing.
- If the bear does attack you, fight back.

A sign warning of bears at the Ceran St. Vrain Trailhead.

38 Susan G. Bretag and Palmer Loop

Garden of the Gods is one of—if not the most—popular natural attractions in Colorado Springs. The impressive red rock formations hold millions of years' worth of history, including remains of the Ancestral Rocky Mountains and layers of gravel, sand, and ocean deposits that the changing landscape left behind over the ages. The formations were uplifted and brought to the surface during a mountain-building event called the Laramide orogeny some 35 to 75 million years ago. The Susan G. Bretag and Palmer Trails loop around the park, passing almost all of the major formations.

Start: Trailhead on north side of main parking lot
Distance: 2.6-mile loop
Difficulty: Easy
Elevation gain: 200 feet
Hiking time: 1–1.5 hours
Trail surface: Dirt and paved walkway
Seasons/schedule: Year-round. May through October, park hours are 5 a.m. to 10 p.m.; November through April, hours are 5 a.m. to 9 p.m.
Fees and permits: None

Other trail users: Mountain bikers or equestrians on some parts of the loop
Canine compatibility: Dogs allowed on leash
Land status: Garden of the Gods Park
Trail contact: Garden of the Gods Park; (719) 634-6666; https://gardenofgods.com/park-info
Maps: National Geographic Trails Illustrated #137: Pikes Peak/Cañon City
Nearest town: Colorado Springs
Cell service: None
Special considerations: None

Finding the trailhead: From the intersection of I-25 and West Cimarron Street (US 24), go west on US 24 for 2.6 miles. Take a slight right toward South 31st Street. In 1.1 mile, turn right onto Water Street and then immediately left onto North 30th Street. After 0.8 mile, take the second exit at the traffic circle onto Gateway Road for 0.4 mile. Turn right on Juniper Way Loop and follow the road around for 0.4 mile to the main parking lot on your left. GPS: N38 52.90' / W104 52.86'

The Hike

In 1859, two surveyors from Denver ventured down to the area that is now Colorado Springs and came upon the towering sandstone formations. M. S. Beach suggested it would be a fantastic place for a "biergarten" as the town developed. According to the park website, his fellow surveyor, Rufus Cable, exclaimed, "Biergarten! Why it is a fit place for the Gods to assemble. We will call it the Garden of the Gods."

The park never turned into a beer garden, but a man named Charles Elliott Perkins—who came to the area to bring the "Q" Railroad to Colorado Springs—purchased 240 acres for a summer home. He decided the natural state was perfect as it was and never built on the property. Before Perkins died in 1907, he made plans for the area to become a public park. His children gave his 480 acres to the City of

The highest formations in the park are near the main parking lot. Jacob Preble

Colorado Springs, under the condition that it "shall remain free to the public, where no intoxicating liquors shall be manufactured, sold, or dispensed, where no building or structure shall be erected except those necessary to properly care for, protect, and maintain the area as a public park." And so it is.

This hike starts on the north side of the main parking lot. Cross the road and climb to the ridges west of the North and South Gateway Rocks. The scenic overview at 0.3 mile is a particularly beautiful spot near sunset because of the way the sun hits the ragged formations, including the North Gateway Rock, the park's highest formation.

Three fun facts about Garden of the Gods:
- It has been voted best city park in the country.
- The only known species of the *Theiophytalia kerri* dinosaur (an herbivorous iguanodontian) was found here by James Kerr in 1878.
- Five different ecosystems come together here: cottonwood-willow, prairie grassland, mountain shrub, pinyon-juniper, and ponderosa pine.

While you won't want to start this hike before sunset, if you time it right you can drive by the scenic overlook around sunset and get the perfect lighting for pictures.

After the overlook, continue west and climb through the piñon and juniper forest. At the high point, you'll have a good view of the Kissing Camels, an arch atop the North Gateway Rock, and the Weeping Indian, a white swath of rock that looks like a face painted onto a darker red rock. Stay straight on the Palmer Trail at 0.8 and 0.9 mile. Pass by the Giant Footprints, piles of horizontal slabs, and then follow the trail parallel to the road. Cross the road at 1.2 miles and go through the picnic area to follow the sandy Scotsman Trail until it hits the road (Juniper Way Loop). Cross the road and join up with the paved Perkins Central Garden Trail to wind through the rest of the formations in the park. Pass Three Spires and Montezuma Tower, popular climbing spots.

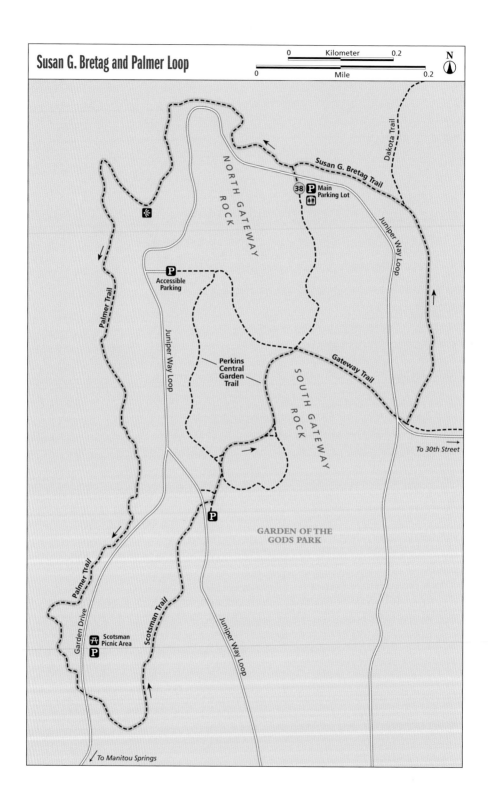

Susan G. Bretag and Palmer Loop

0   Kilometer   0.2
0   Mile   0.2

N

NORTH GATEWAY ROCK

Dakota Trail

Susan G. Bretag Trail

38 Main Parking Lot

Juniper Way Loop

Palmer Trail

Accessible Parking

Juniper Way Loop

Perkins Central Garden Trail

SOUTH GATEWAY ROCK

Gateway Trail

To 30th Street

GARDEN OF THE GODS PARK

Palmer Trail

Garden Drive

Scotsman Trail

Scotsman Picnic Area

Juniper Way Loop

To Manitou Springs

At 2 miles, take a right between the North and South Gateway Rocks on the Gateway Trail. Cross the road and take a left onto the Susan G. Bretag Trail. At 2.4 miles, turn left to follow the trail to the northwest and finish the loop where you started.

Miles and Directions

0.0 Start at the trailhead on the north side of the parking lot.

0.3 Arrive at a scenic overlook.

0.8 Go straight.

0.9 Go straight.

1.2 Cross the road, pass a picnic table, and turn left onto the Scotsman Trail.

1.6 Cross Juniper Way Loop (paved road) and follow the paved Perkins Central Garden Trail.

2.0 Take a right between the North and South Gateway Rocks. Cross the road and turn left on the Susan G. Bretag Trail.

2.4 Come to a junction with the Dakota Trail; turn left and stay to the left.

2.6 Reconnect with the Palmer Trail and arrive back at the trailhead.

Additional Route Options

This route takes you through the major formations in the park. Drive out Garden Lane to Beckers Lane to see the precarious Balanced Rock. As the softer layers of rock near its base were eroded, a larger rock was left on top for the illusion of a rock balancing on a spire.

39 Palmer Trail (Section 16)

Section 16 of the Palmer Trail is one of the best hikes in the Springs. It's challenging in parts, but the terrain varies and mixes exposed sections through thick brush and shaded wooded areas. The views of Colorado Springs, Garden of the Gods, and the foothills to the west are great, especially for a trail so close to town. The last part of the trail follows Bear Creek, where hummingbirds have been known to hang out.

Start: Trailhead at Pulloff 1
Distance: 5.7-mile loop
Difficulty: Strenuous
Elevation gain: 1,325 feet
Hiking time: 2-3 hours
Trail surface: Dirt with some rocky sections
Seasons/schedule: Year-round. May through October, hours are 5 a.m. to 10 p.m.; November through April, hours are 5 a.m. to 9 p.m.
Fees and permits: None
Other trail users: Mountain bikers and equestrians
Canine compatibility: Dogs allowed on leash
Land status: Red Rock Canyon Open Space/ Manitou Section 16 Open Space
Trail contact: Pikes Peak Ranger District; (719) 636-1602;

www.fs.usda.gov/detail/psicc/about-forest/ districts/?cid=fsm9_032731
Maps: National Geographic Trails Illustrated #137: Pikes Peak/Cañon City
Nearest town: Colorado Springs
Cell service: Good
Special considerations: Stay on designated trails; climbing not allowed on the rock formations. Be aware of bears and mountain lions in the area. While it's not likely you'll confront either of them, pay attention to your surroundings, especially early or late in the day. There is a porta-potty by Pulloff 1, but no services at the other parking areas. Part of this trail is exposed and can get warm on hot days, so bring plenty of water.

Finding the trailhead: From the intersection of I-25 and West Cimarron Street (US 24), go west on US 24 for 1.5 miles. Use the left two lanes to turn left onto South 21st Street for 0.8 mile. Turn right onto Lower Gold Camp Road for 1.1 miles. Continue straight onto Gold Camp Road for 0.9 mile until you see the parking lot. There are three parking options here: Pulloff 1 is the main trailhead (on your right, by the Red Rock Canyon Open Space sign) if you hike this trail counterclockwise. Pulloff 3 is farther on the road, straight ahead before the road turns downhill, and is the main trailhead if you hike this trail clockwise. It's also the largest lot. Pulloff 2 is in between the two trailheads, on your left. GPS: N38 49.31' / W104 53.45'

The Hike

Many areas throughout the hills of Colorado Springs were impacted by mining efforts, but Section 16 has been largely undeveloped. It was mined twice—during the Pikes Peak Gold Rush in the 1850s and the uranium boom in the 1950s—and although nothing was found, there are still mineral rights in the gravel. The rights are currently held by the State Land Board.

The steep, rocky section through the ponderosa pines. JACOB PREBLE

The beginning of the trail starts with a narrow path through Gambel oak and other brush.
JACOB PREBLE

There are two ways to hike this trail. If you want a gradual, long (3-plus miles) uphill that avoids the steep uphill section, start at the Pulloff 3 trailhead and hike clockwise. This way starts closer to the hills and winds around and down toward Colorado Springs. The caveat is you have to go down the steep (and sometimes loose) downhill, which can be a little sketchy even with hiking poles. The more popular way to hike this trail is to start at the Pulloff 1 trailhead and proceed counterclockwise. You'll have some very steep sections, but the views get better as you go and then the last 3 miles will be a gradual decline. The directions here are for the counterclockwise route.

Starting from the trailhead, head up several sets of steps as you begin the off-and-on rolling section through the first 2 miles. At the top of the steps are two benches where you can take a break if you'd like, and the trail splits. Stay to the left twice to stay on the main trail. At 0.5 mile, go straight through the junction with the Parallel Trail and Red Rock Overlook Trail. You'll start to notice the red clay trail and red rocks around you (hence the name Red Rock Canyon Open Space), and if you look off to the north, you'll see Garden of the Gods. It's a unique angle to see the iconic red rock formations popping up out of the landscape from a distance, and from above.

This section can get pretty toasty in the summer, as you hike through Gambel oaks and low shrubs that don't give you any shade. Some trail improvements are being made, and the new route will connect the Palmer Trail with the Intemann, Red Rock Overlook, and Parallel Trails. Go straight thorough the soon-to-be intersection to stay on the Palmer Trail. After 0.2 mile, you'll see a V and a sign showing that the Intermittent Waterfall Trail is the higher/right route and the lower/left route goes back to the Palmer Trail, so you'll take a left here.

At 1.3 miles, head left through the forest as you climb a few steep and rocky sections—some of which are over a 20 percent grade. Due to washouts, this section can have some exposed and loose rocks, so watch your footing. At 1.6 miles, stay to the left, following the main, rocky gully. As you approach the top of the trail at almost 8,000 feet, the views open up and you can see the mountains to the southwest, including Mount Arthur and Tenney Crags, and great views of Colorado Springs.

The landscape changes as you round the mountain and start your gradual descent on the other side of this trail. The red clay changes to a pink Pikes Peak granite, and instead of walking though oak shrubs, it's ponderosa pines, yuccas, and grasses lining the trail. Enjoy the gradual descent and take in the views. At 3 miles, you'll cross some rocks over a creek that seems to come out of the large boulder up the hill.

At 4.6 miles, turn left onto the wide, dirt High Drive. Follow it back along Bear Creek and some interesting granite rock formations to Pulloff 3 and then walk up Gold Camp Road to your parking spot.

Miles and Directions

0.0 Start at the trailhead at Pulloff 1.

0.3 Continue straight on the Palmer Trail past the Ridgeline Connector Trail and Meadows Trail.

0.5 Come to a junction with the Parallel Trail and Red Rock Overlook Trail. Stay straight.

0.8 Go straight past the intersection with the Intemann Trail.

1.1 Take the trail to the right.

Gold Camp Road was a former railway known as the Short Line, running from Colorado Springs south to Cripple Creek during the gold rush in the late 1800s. Only part of the road is open to regular vehicles now, as Tunnel #3 collapsed in 1988 and is now the source of many an urban legend. There are nine tunnels total, and the others are reachable by foot, mountain bike, and motorcycle.

Palmer Trail (Section 16)

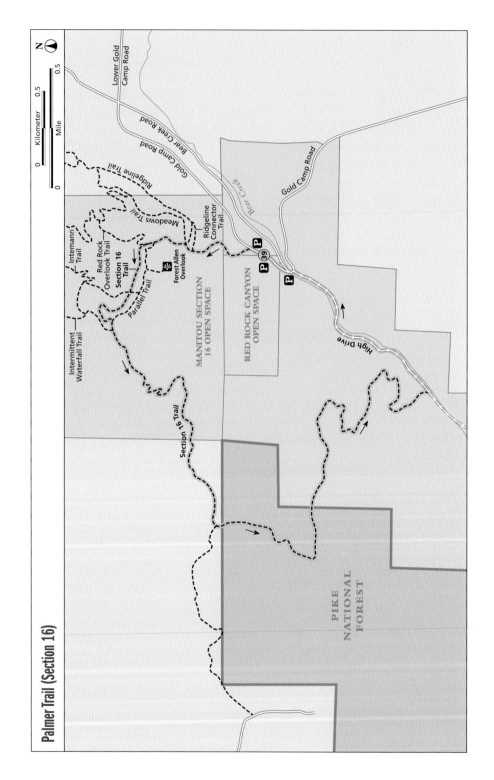

The view from the high point looking southwest. Jacob Preble

1.3 Bear left to stay on the Palmer Trail.

1.3 Head left and uphill.

1.6 Stay left and continue to follow the trail uphill.

2.3 Come around the corner and ignore the unmarked trail coming in from the right; stay on the main trail.

4.6 The Palmer Trail runs into High Drive; turn left and follow it back to the parking lot.

5.7 Arrive back at the trailhead.

Additional Route Options

There are other trails that connect to this one but they all take you farther out. The only spur that could be a nice detour would be the Intermittent Waterfall Trail at 1.3 miles.

40 Fountain Creek Nature Trail

This peaceful trail travels along Fountain Creek, loops around the Cattail Marsh Wildlife Area's wetlands, and meanders back on the Fountain Creek Regional Trail. This easy hike starts and ends in Fountain Creek Regional Park, the perfect spot to spend a summer day with the family (or a few friends!).

Start: Duckwood Trailhead at Fountain Creek Regional Park
Distance: 1.4-mile double loop
Difficulty: Easy
Elevation gain: 36 feet
Hiking time: 0.5–1 hour
Trail surface: Dirt
Seasons/schedule: Year-round. The park and trailhead are open from dawn to dusk.
Fees and permits: None
Other trail users: Mountain bikers

Canine compatibility: Dogs allowed on leash on the Fountain Creek Regional Trail but not in the wildlife area
Land status: El Paso County Parks Trail contact: El Paso County Parks; (970) 520-6375; https://communityservices.elpasoco.com/parks-and-recreation/paint-mines-interpretive -park
Maps: Fountain Creek Regional Park map (available online)
Nearest town: Fountain
Cell service: Good
Special considerations: None

Finding the trailhead: From the intersection of I-25 and West Cimarron Street (US 24), go south on I-25 for 9.2 miles. Take exit 132A to merge onto CO 16/Mesa Ridge Parkway for 1 mile. Take the exit toward US 85 for 0.3 mile, then continue onto North Santa Fe Avenue (US 85/87) for 1.3 miles. Turn right onto Duckwood Road and follow it 0.3 mile to the trailhead parking lot. GPS: N38 42.60' / W104 42.98'

The Hike

The Fountain Creek Regional Trail runs 10.8 miles between the Pikes Peak Greenway Trail and Fountain Creek Regional Park. This section also loops around the Cattail Marsh Wildlife Area and the Nature Center Pond. Over 270 species of birds and more than 40 other wildlife species live and visit the ponds, marsh, woodlands,

Bullsnakes, also known as gopher snakes, are found throughout Colorado, and while their size makes them intimidating (they can grow up to 6 feet long!), they are harmless. They feed mostly on rodents, and though they may hiss or make an S shape to intimidate predators, this snake needs to be seriously provoked to strike. They are nonvenomous, but their bite can still be unpleasant to say the least.

The beginning and the end of the trail follows Fountain Creek. The creekside is forested and the opposite side opens to a meadow.

meadows, and creek. Sixty percent of the state's wildlife depend on wetlands like these. From the cottonwoods to the meadows, the wildlife area offers a great place to look for muskrats, beavers, white-tailed deer, coyotes, and other animals.

Start the hike in the parking lot, cross the bridge, and turn right on the flat, dirt trail. At 0.2 mile, turn right to cross the bridge into the nature area. Turn right, go over another bridge, and then wind around and up to the wildlife viewing area, where you'll have a view of not only the pond but the mountains to the west. Continue down and around the rest of the pond. While you're in the wildlife area, look for some of its residents: blue herons, turtles, white-tailed deer, and bullsnakes.

After you wrap around the pond, take a right, cross the bridge, and turn right to get back on the Fountain Creek Regional Trail. When the trail Vs, bear left to walk through the meadow. It reconnects back at the very first bridge across from the parking lot.

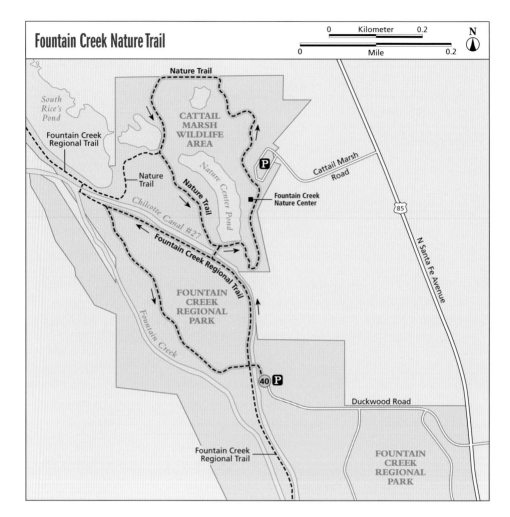

Miles and Directions

0.0 Start at the Duckwood Trailhead. Cross the bridge and go right.

0.2 Turn right; cross a bridge and turn right again.

0.9 Turn right; cross the bridge and turn right onto the Fountain Creek Regional Trail.

1.0 Bear left.

1.3 Reconnect with the beginning of the loop.

1.4 Arrive back at the trailhead.

Additional Route Options

The Fountain Creek Regional Trail runs 10.8 miles one way, so it's possible to add on some mileage here if you'd like.

Bonus Hikes at a Glance

G. Royal Gorge Canyon Rim

This 3.9-mile relatively flat hike is gorgeous, but is mostly exposed and can be hot. It's found within Royal Gorge Park, home of the world's highest suspension bridge towering 956 feet over the Arkansas River, and was the first trail built around the gorge. The trailhead is on CR 3A and is accessible for hikers of all levels. You'll get views of the Sangre de Cristo Mountains to the southwest, Pikes Peak to the north, and the gorge below. You'll have to purchase a ticket to get into the park for this hike, and dogs are allowed on the trails on leash.

Finding the trailhead: From the intersection of I-25 and CO 115, go south on CO 115 for 33 miles. Turn right to merge onto US 50 toward Cañon City for 19.3 miles, then turn left onto CR 3A for 3.6 miles. Turn left on CR 381B into the park. GPS: N38 27.62' / W105 18.79'

H. Mount Muscoco Trail

Running 3.7 miles through North Cheyenne Cañon Park just 10 minutes from town, the Mount Muscoco Trail is a popular trail that has a very challenging 0.5-mile push to the top at just over 8,000 feet in elevation, but otherwise is a manageable hike for most levels along some interesting rock formations. The Mount Muscoco Trail is very easy to follow and is well maintained, just crossing two other trails. Start on the Mount Cutler Trail to mile 0.6. If you want to add a second summit, go straight and add a loop around 7,218-foot Mount Cutler. That adds just under another mile to the total. Otherwise, turn right. Views of Colorado Springs will start to appear in around a mile. At 1.6 miles, turn left to climb Mount Muscoco and take in the views all around you. Return the way you came.

Finding the trailhead: From the intersection of I-25 and CO 115, go south on CO 115 for 0.4 mile. Turn right on East Ramona Avenue for 0.2 mile. At the traffic circle, take the second exit onto Cheyenne Boulevard for 2.5 miles. Take a slight right onto North Cheyenne Canyon Road. The parking area and trailhead will be on the left after 1.5 miles. GPS: N38 47.51' / W104 53.21'

Local Resources and Groups

Action Committee for Eldorado, PO Box 337, Eldorado Springs 80025; www .aceeldo.org

Boulder Ranger District, 2140 Yarmouth Ave., Boulder 80302; (303) 541-2500; www.fs.usda.gov/recarea/arp/recarea/?recid=28178

Clear Creek Ranger District, 101 CO 103, Idaho Springs 80452; (303) 567-4382; www.fs.usda.gov/recarea/arp/recarea/?recid=28372

Colorado Mountain Club, 710 10th St., Ste. 200, Golden 80401; (303) 279-3080; www.cmc.org

Douglas County Open Space, 100 Third St., Castle Rock 80104; (303) 660-7495; www.douglas.co.us/open-space-natural-resources

El Paso County Parks, 2002 Creek Crossing St., Colorado Springs 80905; (970) 520-6375; https://communityservices.elpasoco.com/parks-and-recreation

Friends of Castlewood Canyon State Park, PO Box 403, Franktown 80116; www.castlewoodfriends.org

Friends of Colorado State Parks; www.friendsofcoloradostateparks.com

Friends of Dinosaur Ridge, 16831 W. Alameda Pkwy., Morrison 80465; (303) 697-3466; www.dinoridge.org

Friends of Larimer County Parks and Open Lands, PO Box 2715, Loveland 80539; (970) 619-4570; www.friendsoflarimercounty.org

Indian Peaks Wilderness Alliance; www.indianpeakswilderness.org

Jefferson County Open Space Headquarters, 700 Jefferson County Pkwy., Ste. 100, Golden 80401; (303) 271-5925; www.jeffco.us/open-space

Larimer County Natural Resources, 1800 S. CR 31, Loveland 80537; (970) 619-4570; www.larimer.gov/naturalresources

Pikes Peak Ranger District, 601 S. Weber St., Colorado Springs 80903; (719) 636-1602; www.fs.usda.gov/detail/psicc/about-forest/districts/?cid=fsm9_032731

Rocky Mountain Conservancy, PO Box 3100, Estes Park 80517; (970) 586-0108; www.rmconservancy.org

South Platte Ranger District, 30403 Kings Valley Dr., Ste. 2-115, Conifer 80433; (303) 275-5610; www.fs.usda.gov/recarea/psicc/recarea/?recid=12410

Volunteers for Outdoor Colorado, PO Box 100577, Denver 80250; (303) 715-1010; www.voc.org

Hike Index

Barr Lake Loop—Barr Lake State Park, 93
Beaver Brook and Chavez Trail Loop, 102
Belcher Hill and Mustang Trails, 126
Bergen Peak, 179

Castlewood Canyon State Park Loops, 158
Caribou Ranch Loop, 60
Ceran St. Vrain Trail to Miller Rock, 71
Crater Lakes via South Boulder Creek Trail, 76

Dakota Ridge Trail, 113
Davidson Mesa Open Space, 37
Devil's Backbone Loop, 9
Devil's Head Lookout Trail, 172
Dream and Emerald Lakes Trail—Rocky Mountain National Park, 18

Evergreen Mountain Trail, 131

Finch Lake via Allenspark Trail—Rocky Mountain National Park, 31
Flatirons Vista Trail, 85
Fountain Creek Nature Trail, 202

Grays and Torreys Peaks, 148
Green Mountain via Gregory Canyon and Ranger Trails, 89

Horsetooth Falls Loop, 3

Lake Haiyaha Loop—Rocky Mountain National Park, 22
Lake Isabelle via Pawnee Pass Trail, 65
Lory State Park, 14
Lost Lake via Hessie Trail, 90
Lost Pond Loop—Mueller State Park, 186

Mount Falcon Park Upper Loop, 107
Mount Galbraith Loop via Cedar Gulch Trail, 117
Mount Muscoco Trail, 205

O'Fallon Park Loop, 178
Ouzel Falls via Wild Basin Trail—Rocky Mountain National Park, 27

Paint Mines Interpretive Park, 182
Palmer Trail (Section 16), 196
Peaks to Plains Trail—Gateway Trailhead, 122
Poudre River Trail, 15

Raccoon Trail—Golden Gate Canyon State Park, 97
Rattlesnake Gulch Trail—Eldorado Canyon State Park, 81
Royal Arch Trail, 46
Royal Gorge Canyon Rim, 205

Sandstone Meadow Loop, 168
South Park 600 Trail to Square Top Lakes, 154
South Rim and Willow Creek Trails—Roxborough State Park, 163
St. Mary's Glacier and James Peak, 144
Staunton Ranch, Old Mill, and Border Line Trails—Staunton State Park, 138
Sugarloaf Mountain, 52
Sunny Aspen Trail and Lodge Pole Loop, 135
Susan G. Bretag and Palmer Loop, 191

Walker Ranch Loop, 41
Wapiti and Ponderosa Loop Trails, 55

THE TEN ESSENTIALS OF HIKING

American Hiking Society

American Hiking Society recommends you pack the "Ten Essentials" every time you head out for a hike. Whether you plan to be gone for a couple of hours or several months, make sure to pack these items. Become familiar with these items and know how to use them.

1. Appropriate Footwear
Happy feet make for pleasant hiking. Think about traction, support, and protection when selecting well-fitting shoes or boots.

2. Navigation
While phones and GPS units are handy, they aren't always reliable in the backcountry; consider carrying a paper map and compass as backups and know how to use them.

3. Water (and a way to purify it)
As a guideline, plan for half a liter of water per hour in moderate temperatures/terrain. Carry enough water for your trip and know where and how to treat water while you're out on the trail.

4. Food
Pack calorie-dense foods to help fuel your hike, and carry an extra portion in case you are out longer than expected.

5. Rain Gear & Dry-Fast Layers
The weatherman is not always right. Dress in layers to adjust to changing weather and activity levels. Wear moisture-wicking clothes and carry a warm hat.

6. Safety Items (light, fire, and a whistle)
Have means to start an emergency fire, signal for help, and see the trail and your map in the dark.

7. First Aid Kit
Supplies to treat illness or injury are only as helpful as your knowledge of how to use them. Take a class to gain the skills needed to administer first aid and CPR.

8. Knife or Multi-Tool
With countless uses, a multi-tool can help with gear repair and first aid.

9. Sun Protection
Sunscreen, sunglasses, and sun-protective clothing should be used in every season regardless of temperature or cloud cover.

10. Shelter
Protection from the elements in the event you are injured or stranded is necessary. A lightweight, inexpensive space blanket is a great option.

Find other helpful resources at AmericanHiking.org/hiking-resources.